INSTITUTE OF PSYCHIATRY

Maudsley Monographs

PSYCHIATRIC DIAGNOSIS IN NEW YORK AND LONDON

INSTITUTE OF PSYCHIATRY

MAUDSLEY MONOGRAPHS

Number Twenty

PSYCHIATRIC DIAGNOSIS IN NEW YORK AND LONDON

A Comparative Study of Mental Hospital Admissions

BY

J. E. COOPER   R. E. KENDELL
M.R.C.P., D.P.M.   M.D., M.R.C.P., D.P.M.

B. J. GURLAND   L. SHARPE   J. R. M. COPELAND
M.R.C.P., D.P.M.   M.B., D.P.M.   M.R.C.P., D.P.M.

R. SIMON
M.A.

THE UNITED STATES—UNITED KINGDOM
DIAGNOSTIC PROJECT

Biometrics Research
The New York State Department of Mental Hygiene, New York
and
The Institute of Psychiatry, London

LONDON
OXFORD UNIVERSITY PRESS
NEW YORK   TORONTO
1972

Oxford University Press, Ely House, London W. 1

GLASGOW   NEW YORK   TORONTO   MELBOURNE   WELLINGTON
CAPE TOWN   IBADAN   NAIROBI   DAR ES SALAAM   LUSAKA   ADDIS ABABA
DELHI   BOMBAY   CALCUTTA   MADRAS   KARACHI   LAHORE   DACCA
KUALA LUMPUR   SINGAPORE   HONG KONG   TOKYO

ISBN 0 19 712142 X

PRINTED IN GREAT BRITAIN
AT THE UNIVERSITY PRESS, OXFORD
BY VIVIAN RIDLER
PRINTER TO THE UNIVERSITY

CONTENTS

PART 4. CONCLUSIONS

THE STAFF OF THE UNITED STATES–UNITED KINGDOM DIAGNOSTIC PROJECT

NATIONAL INSTITUTE OF HEALTH GRANT MH–09191

PRINCIPAL INVESTIGATOR: J. Zubin, Ph.D.

The studies described in this monograph were carried out by the following teams:

NEW YORK TEAM

B. J. Gurland, M.R.C.P., D.P.M.
(*Deputy Director*)
L. Sharpe, M.B., D.P.M.
*T. Farkas, M.D.
R. J. Simon, M.A.
P. Roberts
V. Hoff, M.A.

LONDON TEAM

J. E. Cooper, M.R.C.P., D.P.M.
(*Deputy Director*)
R. E. Kendell, M.D., M.R.C.P., D.P.M.
J. R. M. Copeland, M.R.C.P., D.P.M.
†N. Sartorius, M.D.
A. J. Gourlay, M.A.
†M. E. David, B.A.
†A. Vickery
*G. Stoneham
*B. S. Everitt, B.SC., M.SC.

* Part-time member of the project team
† Participated only in the Brooklyn–Netherne Study

ADVISORY COMMITTEE

J. Zubin
P. Hoch (until 1967)
M. Kramer
H. Lehmann (from 1967)
A. Miller (from 1970)
B. Pasamanick

UNITED STATES STEERING COMMITTEE

B. J. Gurland
M. Kramer
R. L. Spitzer
J. Zubin

UNITED KINGDOM STEERING COMMITTEE

M. Shepherd
A. J. Lewis (*Psychiatric Consultant*)
J. K. Wing
J. E. Cooper

MAUDSLEY MONOGRAPHS

HENRY MAUDSLEY, from whom this series of monographs takes its name, was the founder of The Maudsley Hospital and the most prominent English psychiatrist of his generation. The Maudsley Hospital is now united with the Bethlem Royal Hospital and its medical school, renamed the Institute of Psychiatry, has become part of the British Postgraduate Medical Federation. It is entrusted by the University of London with the duty to advance psychiatry by teaching and research.

The monograph series reports work carried out in the Institute and in the associated Hospital. Some of the monographs are directly concerned with clinical problems; others, less obviously relevant, are in scientific fields that are cultivated for the furtherance of psychiatry.

Joint Editors

PROFESSOR SIR DENIS HILL
F.R.C.P., D.P.M.

PROFESSOR G. S. BRINDLEY
M.D., M.R.C.P., F.R.S.

with the assistance of
MISS S. E. HAGUE
B.Sc. (Econ.), M.A.

PREFACE

THE investigation reported in this book, like the mental disorders which were studied, had many origins and was the result of the thinking and application of many individuals. Historically it is difficult to trace who first promulgated the idea that different countries or cultures had different rates of mental disorder, although perhaps the classic reference to higher rates of madness in England is to be found in Hamlet: ' 'T'will not be seen in him there; there the men are as mad as he.' More recently, the differences known to exist between the United States and the United Kingdom in psychiatric admission rates have been discussed at various times by Drs. Lewis, Shepherd, Kramer, and Zubin, and out of these informal discussions several of the ideas of the cross-national study emerged. If there was a single person who might be said to have been the prime mover in the actual implementation of the current study, it was Dr. Morton Kramer who nurtured the early development of the proposal and gave it encouragement. Another man to whom the project owed much in its initial development was the late Dr. Paul H. Hoch who protected it in its formative stages and lent it the international prestige which attracted the co-operation of Sir Aubrey Lewis and his colleagues at the Institute of Psychiatry at the Maudsley Hospital, as well as the necessary financial assistance from the National Institute of Mental Health.

My own part in the project was born as a consequence of two events. First, I was offered a Fellowship by the Commonwealth Fund, soon after the Biometrics Research Unit was established. The Fellowship award was to defray the expenses of visiting various research centres in Europe and Israel where epidemiologic and biometric studies of the mental disorders were under way. It soon became evident that, although the same terms and labels were used in different centres, agreement on their significance and meaning was not universal. As a consequence, a proposal was made to NIMH for convening a work conference under the auspices of the American Psychopathological Association and Biometrics Research to consider the possibility of introducing a more uniform vocabulary and a more comparable classification system. The results of this conference were reported in a volume under my editorship, *Field Studies in the Mental Disorders* (Hoch and Zubin, 1961). Finally, it became clear that conferences would not settle the matter and that a field study was required. With the help of Dr. Kramer, a special application to NIMH was prepared by a committee consisting of Drs. Paul H. Hoch, Benjamin Pasamanick, and the writer. This special grant was awarded to begin in 1963.

The first 2 years were spent in organizing staff, reviewing the literature, and developing co-operation between the United Kingdom representatives and the United States Steering Committee. Preliminary meetings were held in 1964 in London between this Steering Committee and a British group consisting of

Professor Sir Aubrey Lewis and Dr. Michael Shepherd of the Institute of Psychiatry, Miss Eileen Brooke (Ministry of Health), Dr. A. B. Monro (Secretary, Royal Medico-Psychological Association), Dr. R. Doll (Medical Research Council), and Dr. J. E. Cooper. For the purpose of a further series of meetings in 1965, two larger committees were formed, expert advice being obtained from Dr. J. Fleiss, Dr. E. Burdock, Dr. A. Hardesty and Dr. R. Spitzer of the Biometrics Department, New York State Psychiatric Institute, and from Dr. D. L. Davies, Dr. John Wing and Professor A. E. Maxwell of the Institute of Psychiatry. Backing up the efforts of the New York team, headed by Dr. Barry Gurland, was the entire staff of Biometrics Research, especially Dr. Muriel Hammer, Head of Anthropology Section; Dr. Ruth Bennett, Head of Sociology Section; Dr. Samuel Sutton, Deputy Chief of Biometrics Research and Head of Psychophysiology Section. The London team, headed by Dr. John Cooper, was aided by the statistical unit of Professor A. E. Maxwell, and continued to collaborate closely with the Social Psychiatry Research Unit of the Medical Research Council (Director: Professor John Wing), with whom some early work on the development of a standardized mental state interview had already been done.

This project has developed several interests in addition to the hospital admission studies described in this monograph. One of its primary concerns became the degree of agreement in rating and diagnostic behaviour among different clinicians when viewing the same interview. To facilitate this investigation, a videotape studio was developed in each country and installed in special mobile units so that it could be transported from hospital to hospital for the purpose of videotaping patients, as well as displaying them to audiences of raters. Some of this work is summarized here in relation to the hospital study but it is reported in detail elsewhere.

Another activity of the project has been to stimulate interest in the development of objective physiological indicators of psychopathology which might eventually supplement interviews as aids to diagnosis. With the help of Drs. Samuel Sutton and Mitchell Kietzman of Biometrics Research, a conference was held in 1968 in New York attended by an internationally representative group of psychophysiologists and behavioural scientists interested in psychopathology, the proceedings of which are to be published.

While it is too early to tell what impact our findings will eventually have on the diagnosis, classification, treatment, and outcome of mental illness in both countries, it is already clear that we have succeeded in at least one respect. The variation we have demonstrated between the two countries in labelling the same types of patients has brought the problem of diagnosis to the fore in both, and judging from the interest displayed in our findings we may see a renewed interest in classification and in correlation of treatment with psychopathology.

We have discharged our first set of responsibilities—investigating the reasons for the discrepancy in the admission rates for mental disorders, especially schizophrenia and affective disorders, between London and New York in the adult age range (20–59). We now approach the more difficult task of trying to unravel the causes of the differences in the disorders of the senium. We hope that, given the co-operation and support we enjoyed thus far, this task will prove as productive as the first and result in improved diagnosis, classification, treatment, and outcome for elderly patients in both countries.

J. ZUBIN

New York, 1971

ACKNOWLEDGEMENTS

IT is a pleasure to record our gratitude to the staff and patients of the many hospitals whose co-operation enabled this study to be performed, and in particular to Brooklyn State Hospital (Medical Superintendent, the late Dr. Nathan Beckenstein) and to Netherne Hospital (Medical Superintendent, Dr. R. K. Freudenberg). In New York the other State hospitals which granted us facilities for the sampling survey were Bronx, Creedmoor, Central Islip, King's Park, Manhattan, Pilgrim, Rockland, and the Psychiatric Institute, and in London the other area mental hospitals involved were Bexley, Claybury, Friern, Goodmayes, Long Grove, St. Bernard's, Shenley, Warley, and West Park.

Invaluable help and advice was obtained from both individuals and groups of workers in the parent Institutes where the two teams were based. In New York, Drs. R. Spitzer, J. Endicott, and J. Cohen gave special assistance with data handling and analyses related to the Psychiatric Status Schedule and Diagno I, and Dr. J. Fleiss provided extensive programming and statistical help on many occasions. In London, statistical advice and help was given by Professor A. E. Maxwell and Mr. B. Everitt. Dr. W. E. Deming provided expert counsel on sampling and statistical methods to both teams. Dr. M. G. Sandifer, Jr. participated in the early stages of planning but left the Project before the field work of this study began.

Particular thanks are due to the New York State Department of Mental Hygiene, and the Ministry of Health (now Department of Health and Social Security) in London. As the official collecting and publishing agencies for admission statistics, these two bodies co-operated generously throughout the period of study and allowed us access to much of their data. Miss Gillian Cutting, the Project Secretary in London, typed the manuscript of this volume with her customary speed and accuracy, and we are indebted to her for this and many other clerical tasks performed so well over the last few years.

Finally, the authors of this volume would like to acknowledge the part played by their senior colleagues, particularly Dr. J. Zubin, Sir Aubrey Lewis, Dr. M. Kramer, the late Dr. P. Hoch, Professor M. Shepherd, and Professor J. K. Wing. This study, and the other work of the Diagnostic Project, would not have been possible without their sustained interest and efforts over many years.

Both the New York and the London teams were supported by Public Health Service grant MH–09191 from the National Institute of Mental Health in the United States.

London, 1971

PART 1. INTRODUCTORY

CHAPTER I

CLASSIFICATION AND DIAGNOSIS IN PSYCHIATRY: A HISTORICAL NOTE

SIR AUBREY LEWIS

A PROMINENT German psychiatrist of the last century, Heinrich Neumann, ranked classification high: 'It expresses our insight into the essential nature and development of the object classified' (Neumann, 1883). He propounded a classificatory schema based on symptoms and the stages through which they pass; one comprehensive disease taking different forms. 'This way of looking at the matter', he wrote, 'is important for psychiatric progress. Consider its bearing on statistics. A prime requirement for any statistic is that the units on which the calculation rests should be identical. If a statistical problem is to be solved, the result of the calculations is precisely nil, if the units are not identical. Indeed it is worse than nothing because its errors are paraded and spread in the resplendent attire of mathematics.'

Here, two crucial, still unsettled issues are stated: first, the 'diagnostic entity' problem; and secondly, how to ensure that in observation and enumeration we deal with identical units, permitting epidemiological comparison.

The setting up of an orderly and consistent table of 'diagnostic entities' has long been a bugbear of psychiatry. 'The wit of man', wrote Hack Tuke, 'has rarely been more exercised than in the attempt to classify the morbid phenomena covered by the term "insanity".' Classification has remained a battlefield, strewn with conflicting notions of 'disease', 'syndrome', 'type of reaction', 'symptom complex', and the like. Neumann, in agreement with Zeller (1844) and Griesinger (1845), plumped with simplifying ardour for one mental disorder, or disease, which changed shape as it progressed: beginning as depression, it could turn to mania (*Tollheit*), delusional forms (*Wahnsinn, Verrücktheit*), and finally to dementia (*Blödsinn*).

The concept of one comprehensive mental disease (*die Einheitspsychose*) thus launched a century ago has maintained a sporadic life, with various modifications, into the present time (Llopis, 1954; Conrad, 1959; Menninger, 1963). It no longer allocates diverse forms of the single illness to diverse stages but now leans heavily on psychopathology. Still, with rare exceptions, its proponents concede the necessity to classify the phenomena, whether the process is called diagnosis or not.

A classification schema will fail if it has been intended to serve conflicting purposes. Neumann foresaw the consequences that might ensue from muddled parameters: 'Better no classification than a bad one.' This was too radical a view, as the course of events has shown; some classification is essential, to escape chaos. But reviews like those of Ey (1954), J. E. Meyer (1961), Brill (1966), Zubin (1967), and Cohen (1970) record the intellectual straits to which the necessity to classify has reduced many thoughtful and erudite psychiatrists during the last two centuries.

An aetiological classification of mental illnesses was the ideal for which many psychiatrists vainly longed. Arnold wrote in 1782, 'When the science of causes shall be complete we may then make them the basis of our classification, but till then we ought to content ourselves with an arrangement according to symptoms' (Arnold, 1782). Prichard, not long after, declared that 'an aetiological classification is the only mode of terminology and arrangement that can be of any practical advantage, and this is all we have to consult' (Prichard, 1835). Gradually it came to be recognized that there are here two major obstacles: the aetiology of many important forms of mental illnesses is not known, and the causes of every mental illness (where they are known) are multiple. Among the multiple causes one may be singled out as necessary, or immediate (precipitating), or preponderant, or genetic; but to make it then the sole criterion of a classificatory axis is impracticable.

In spite of the powerful objections to more than one principle of division being applied within one scheme, the current classification (*International Classification of Diseases*, 8) is a hotch-potch of classifications by cause, pathology, course, and clinical pattern. It is an empirical utilitarian scheme such as Hughlings Jackson contrasted with a scientific one. Parented by Kahlbaum (1863) and Kraepelin (1887, 1927), it was—and to some extent still is—influenced by somatic paradigms. It flies in the face of taxonomic rectitude, but persists for lack of anything better which would be generally acceptable. Its defects could be lessened by direct action (such as the two World Health Organization programmes) as well as by advances in our knowledge of causes and pathology. More logical classifications (such as Essen-Möller's proposed dual system (Essen-Möller and Wohlfart, 1947)) have failed because they did not accord with ingrained diagnostic habits.

In psychiatry more than in any other branch of medicine it is difficult to delimit what is morbid from what is healthy. On this may turn the decision as to whether treatment is to be instituted, or whether legal sanctions rather than medical therapies are called for. There is, however, much diversity in different psychiatrists' standpoints regarding the boundaries of normality. There is a similar diversity in determining what are the desiderata for assigning an illness to one of the ideal types of reaction, syndrome, pattern, entity, or whatever else it may be called. As Adolf Meyer put it over 50 years ago, 'We should have our concepts and words for the totalities, even if they can never be fully realized as wholly indisputable entities. For both scientific and

In the meanwhile, 'the best rule, however, for everybody to observe when attempting to form a judgement on any particular case of insanity, is to take care and preserve his own faculties clear, and as free from the mysticisms of speculative philosophy as from the trammels of nosology' (Burrows, 1828).

CHAPTER II

THE BACKGROUND TO THE STUDY

THIS study is concerned with the diagnostic meaning of routinely collected mental hospital statistics, and its design allows comparisons to be made between statistics arising from area mental hospitals in London and State hospitals in New York. Psychiatric statistics have not been a popular subject for study in the past, although marked differences have been known to exist between the United States and Great Britain in this field for many years. One striking example of these differences will serve to indicate the field of interest of this work, before moving on to an introductory discussion of two issues with which this study is concerned, namely, statistics relating to mental illness, and the reliability of diagnosis in psychiatry.

Figures prepared by Kramer (Kramer, 1961, 1969a and b) showed that the mental hospital first-admission rate for England and Wales for manic-depressive psychosis (or reaction) in the age-group 55–64 years was about 20 times the corresponding American rate. This difference is so large that it demands an explanation. Possible contributors to the disparity are differences between the two parent populations in hospital utilization and in biological and genetic constitution, and the presence of different ecological influences. Before an investigation into any of these, or other, possibilities is justified it is necessary to establish what proportion of the differences in reported statistics can be attributed to the patients themselves. If the patients on two sides of the Atlantic turned out to be very similar to one another when both were assessed by the same methods, one would be forced to conclude that the reported diagnostic differences were, at least in part, artifacts produced by differences in diagnostic criteria. Such a finding could hardly fail to be of interest to those concerned with the collection and use of statistics, and would also raise the question of whether psychiatrists are entitled to accept at face value diagnostic statements in psychiatric investigations carried out in countries other than their own. Thus, an examination of this statistical disparity appeared to be worthwhile whatever the results.

NATIONAL STATISTICS OF MENTAL ILLNESS

The importance and usefulness of statistics relating to mental illness have been recognized by prominent psychiatric writers for over 100 years, so it is surprising that so little is known about their deficiencies. In the introduction to his *Study of the Major Psychoses in an English County*, Shepherd (1957) traces briefly the history of the recognition of the importance of psychiatric statistics, starting with Prichard (1835), Esquirol (1838), and Thurnham

(1845), and culminating in the British nationwide system of collection made possible by the inception of the National Health Service in 1948, upon which his own study was based. The most prominent early studies in this field were not carried out in Great Britain, and Shepherd instances workers in other countries, such as Ødegaard (1945, 1946) and Svendsen (1952) in Scandinavia, and Pollock and Malzberg (1937) in the United States. More recently, the World Health Organization, with its international responsibilities, has brought together published psychiatric statistics from many different countries (World Health Organization, 1963; 1966; 1968). These and many other studies provide ample evidence for the usefulness of routinely collected psychiatric statistics, but it must not be forgotten that until very recently the type of information used was quite limited, in that the statistics regularly available were concerned only with admissions to mental hospitals or psychiatric out-patient clinics. Even in 1969, Kramer felt obliged to begin an extensive review of contemporary statistics of mental disorders in the United States with the statement: 'Annual morbidity statistics on the prevalence and incidence of mental disorders are not available for the United States or for any other country' (Kramer, 1969b).

In the majority of published studies, there are no more than passing comments on the quality of the psychiatric diagnoses being used, and in particular there has been insufficient emphasis upon the presence of two distinct components in psychiatric statistics as they are usually collected. There is first of all a group of 'hard facts' such as age, sex, marital status, and length of stay in hospital; however these are collected they are likely to be comparatively reliable. With the second component, a diagnosis, quite different problems are encountered, due mainly to variations in diagnostic habits among psychiatrists. Every psychiatrist is familiar, at an anecdotal level, with the diagnostic differences that can occur between himself and his colleagues under ordinary clinical conditions. In the context of clinical work or teaching activities, these differences are often stimulating and productive of useful discussion, but for statistical purposes they are merely sources of variation which must be minimized.

Part of the explanation for this lack of appreciation of the inherent problems of psychiatric diagnosis may lie in the fact that those responsible for the collection and compilation of psychiatric statistics are usually administrators and statisticians. Experienced clinical psychiatrists who might be expected to be only too familiar with the problems have tended to neglect this field. Probably the most widespread manifestation of this indifference is the reluctance of many hospital clinicians in Great Britain to follow the repeated requests of the Ministry of Health to use the nomenclature of the *International Classification of Diseases* when making official hospital admission diagnoses for the monthly statistical returns.

It seems reasonable to accept that large-scale psychiatric statistics contain information potentially of great interest for epidemiology and for purposes of planning and administration, but their acceptance must be qualified by inquiry into the extent and sources of the inevitable variations, and by constructive criticism to improve their quality. Uncritical acceptance of their diagnostic value, as in the studies by Burch (1964a and b), must mean that the authors' conclusions will be at least as suspect as the quality of the diagnoses themselves.

There are signs, however, that more attention is being paid to the quality of psychiatric statistics, as a result of the increasing emphasis in the last two decades upon the rational planning of psychiatric services. The complex system of different types of treatment and care that forms the current ideal of a comprehensive psychiatric service needs careful planning to make the most of the usually inadequate resources available. It becomes necessary to estimate numbers and types of patients for very practical reasons, and since the deployment of manpower and money will depend directly upon such estimates, they must be based upon reliable information.

The need for reliable diagnostic methods and for the consistent use of psychiatric terms, which are central features of the present study, is now only too apparent.

THE RELIABILITY OF PSYCHIATRIC DIAGNOSIS

There is a good deal of evidence to show that under ordinary clinical conditions psychiatric diagnosis is usually an unreliable procedure. The whole problem of this unreliability will not be reviewed here in full, since several fairly recent commentaries have covered the subject (Kreitman, 1961; Beck, 1962; Zubin, 1967). It is, however, worthwhile selecting a number of studies which illustrate the different types of inter-psychiatrist variation that can influence diagnostic statistics.

In one recent experimental study, the sources of variation were conveniently summarized as 'first, variations at the level of observation and perception by the clinician; secondly, variations in the inferences drawn from such observations; and thirdly, variations in the nosological schemata employed by the individual clinicians' (Shepherd, Brooke, Cooper, and Lin, 1968). Good examples of variations between observers at the perceptual level were obtained by Katz, Cole, and Lowery (1969) who showed short cine films of psychiatric interviews to audiences of psychiatrists. For two of the patients used, the audiences showed significant variations in their ratings of 'apathy', in spite of the use of a rating method that ensured that all the raters used the same simply-phrased rating-scales (Lorr and Klett, 1967). High ratings on apathy were associated with a diagnosis of schizophrenia, which raises the question of how early in an interview is a diagnosis made by the clinician, and how much does this affect his subsequent judgements and perceptions. One of Katz's films was shown in both the United States and in London, and the American psychiatrists had a significantly lower threshold for the perception of abnormal behaviour and symptoms than the British.

This finding was confirmed by another transatlantic comparison (Sandifer, Hordern, Timbury, and Green, 1969). During a series of evaluations of 23 American patients by eight British and 33 American psychiatrists, Sandifer and his colleagues found that the American psychiatrists reported almost twice as many symptoms as the British. A complete cross-over rating experiment in which psychiatrists from two or more cultures all rate in turn patients from the same cultures has not yet been reported, but even without this it seems very likely that these two groups of workers have encountered a difference in rating sensitivity between British and American psychiatrists which will prove to be important and widespread.

The final stage in the diagnostic process, that of choosing a term from a nomenclature, is particularly vulnerable to individual differences between diagnosticians, as shown by the study of Ward, Beck, Mendelson, Mock, and Erbaugh (1962). This study was directly aimed at identifying and estimating the relative importance of different sources of inter-observer variation while using the *Diagnostic and Statistical Manual: Mental Disorders* (DSM I) (American Psychiatric Association, 1952). Each of a series of 153 patients was seen and diagnosed separately by two different psychiatrists who then met to discuss and identify the sources of disagreement in the 40 cases where this had occurred. They concluded that the causes of disagreement were:

1. Inadequacy of the nosology, responsible for 62·5 per cent of the disagreement (25 cases).
2. Inconsistency on the part of the diagnostician, responsible for 32·5 per cent of the disagreement (13 cases).
3. Inconsistency on the part of the patient, responsible for 5 per cent of the disagreement (2 cases).

By 'inadequacies of the nosology' they meant that they found that descriptions of diagnostic categories were sometimes overlapping and not mutually exclusive, and that there were inadequate instructions and guidance about how to give precedence to one disorder when two or more were judged to be present. In other words, even with a conscientious effort to follow the *Manual*, too much was still left to be decided by individual attitudes and preferences.

In most of the reported studies of the unreliability of psychiatric diagnosis, it is not possible to apportion out the demonstrated variations to the different components of the diagnostic process; they show only a total sum of variations from all possible sources. Such studies are valuable none the less, since they illustrate how much variation can occur in widely different settings, whether experimental or clinical.

Studies done within the setting of one hospital can bring to light a surprising amount of variation between clinicians. One such study was reported by Pasamanick, Dinitz, and Lefton (1959), but it does not seem to have aroused the attention it deserves, perhaps because of the disarming simplicity of its design. It consists merely of a description of the routine hospital diagnoses made upon 538 female patients entering the wards of a well-staffed University hospital. The patients went into one of three wards with little or no selection between wards. The three resulting groups of patients did not differ in a variety of personal characteristics such as age, race, and socio-economic status, so there was no reason to suppose that their diagnostic breakdowns would be very different. In fact, very marked differences in the distribution of major diagnostic categories were found and could be traced to the individual ideas of the three psychiatrists in charge of the sections. For instance, one psychiatrist made a diagnosis of schizophrenia in 66 per cent of his patients, the others in 22 per cent and 29 per cent. For 'character disorders' one psychiatrist put 57 per cent of his patients into this group, a second 47 per cent, and the third only 15 per cent. This study is important because the authors were able to show that these variations in diagnostic habits were not merely of academic interest but were associated with differences in treatment. Nor do they mince their words in summarizing their conclusions: '. . . despite protestations that their point of reference is always the individual patient, clinicians in fact may be so committed to a particular psychiatric school of thought that the patient's diagnosis and treatment is largely predetermined'.

The stability of diagnosis over time has been the subject of some interest as another aspect of reliability, although a change in the clinical state of the patient is always a possible complication. A 1-year follow-up study of 100 patients studied in considerable detail (Masserman and Carmichael, 1938) is often quoted as a source of evidence for the unreliability of psychiatric diagnosis, since 41 of the patients required a revision of the diagnosis at the end of the year. It is, however, impossible to tell from the method of study whether the changes resulted from change in the patients, or from differing diagnostic habits among the clinicians concerned. In addition, examination of the details of the changes shows that some categories were quite stable; for instance 15 out of 18 patients called 'organic psychoses' kept the same diagnosis, as did seven out of eight labelled 'manic-depressive psychosis'. The categories of 'adult maladjustment', and the neuroses, were responsible for most of the instability, for only 18 patients out of 45 in these two groups kept their original diagnosis. Schizophrenia was intermediate in its stability. Such a wide range of variation makes generalizations unjustified, but rather points to the need for further studies on the stability of the individual categories.

There is evidence from a British study that changes in doctor produce most changes in diagnosis over time. The mental hospital admission statistics collected by the Ministry of Health since 1948 have made possible a large-scale longitudinal study (Brooke, 1963), and from the 44,047 patients in this group who had their first admission in 1954 a group of 200 were selected who had four admissions within 2 years of their first (Cooper, 1967). It might be expected that in the majority of these patients the admissions would all be for the same condition, but according to the 3-digit categories of the *International Classification of Diseases* (Seventh Edition) into which the diagnoses were grouped, only 37 per cent retained the same diagnosis throughout. By regrouping the diagnoses into eight broad groupings (Schizophrenia, Affective Disorders, Neuroses, Personality Disorders, etc.) and by subjecting the case-notes of each admission to a uniform assessment procedure by one psychiatrist, the proportion of patients keeping the same diagnosis rose to 81 per cent. Strong correlations were also evident between the number of changes in diagnosis and the number of changes of doctor. This study was comparatively crude in that it relied upon the assessment of case-notes, but the sheer size of the reduction in diagnostic changes is impressive.

In view of the length of time that this evidence of the unreliability of psychiatric diagnosis has been common knowledge, it is surprising that the problem was not investigated at an international level prior to the recent work of Sandifer and his colleagues (Sandifer, Hordern, Timbury, and Green, 1968). These authors carried out a series of diagnostic comparisons between 33 psychiatrists in North Carolina, four in London and four in Glasgow. Their study used cine films of 30 brief clinical psychiatric interviews, supported by a written summary of the patient's psychiatric, social, and family history and the results of psychological and laboratory investigations. The differences between the diagnoses of British and American psychiatrists were not very striking and were not in accordance with expectations from Kramer's statistics (Kramer, 1969a), for the British and North Carolina groups used the diagnosis of schizophrenia to the same extent (for the North Carolina psychiatrists 18 per cent of all diagnoses, compared with 16 per cent for the British). For manic-depressive psychosis, however, the findings were more in line with expectation, the British psychiatrists using this term twice as often as their American counterparts. In addition, the North Carolina group used the term 'neurotic depressive' far more than the British groups, and the Glasgow group alone made particular use of 'personality disorder'. The diagnosticians in North Carolina were apparently typical of their local colleagues, for the authors comment that the 18 per cent of diagnoses of schizophrenia made by the North Carolina psychiatrists is close to the annual percentage of admissions so diagnosed at their parent hospital. The existence of regional differences in admission rates or diagnostic criteria is an obvious possibility in a country as large and varied as the United States, and may account for the disparity between the results of this study and Kramer's. The issue is considered further in CHAPTER XVIII.

In contrast, one of the studies reported by Katz, Cole, and Lowery (1969) revealed a very large Anglo-American diagnostic difference for schizophrenia, at least for the one patient involved. A filmed psychiatric interview was shown to 42 American and to 32 British psychiatrists: the patient was an attractive young woman in her middle twenties with a variety of fairly mild symptoms of anxiety and depression, who also complained of difficulty with inter-personal relationships and the frustration of her ambition to be an actress. In spite of one-third of the American psychiatrists making a diagnosis of schizophrenia, none of the British put this forward as the primary diagnosis. The predilection of American psychiatrists for symptoms related to or suggestive of schizophrenia was shown by the use of the terms schizophrenia and schizoid personality by nearly half of them, whereas over half of the British psychiatrists used diagnoses with a more affective connotation such as depressive neurosis or emotionally unstable personality. Another experiment reported in the same paper showed how wide a variety of diagnoses can be given to a single patient; 44 American psychiatrists between them used 12 different diagnoses after all viewing the same film.

This last example from the work of Katz shows how marked the contribution of individual differences between diagnosticians can be towards variation in psychiatric diagnosis, since all the psychiatrists in both countries received exactly the same information and recorded their observations according to the same instructions. Because of the lack of objective or quantifiable data, there is no doubt that of all branches of medicine, psychiatry is most prone to this hazard. But this necessary examination of glaring examples taken from psychiatry must not obscure the presence of a good deal of inter-observer disagreement in many investigations used in general medicine that are usually accepted without question as objective and reliable. Beck, for instance, lists the assessment of emphysema, judgements on the nutritional state of children, estimates of the degree of pathological inflammation of tonsils, and accounts of pulmonary symptoms in medical history taking, as examples of medical procedures that have all been shown to be subject to significant inter-observer error (Beck, 1962). Other examples are the assessment of X-ray films (Garland, 1960), blood pressure readings by sphygmomanometer (Oldham, Pickering, Roberts, and Sowry, 1960; Holland, 1963), and the interpretation of ECGs (Kagan, 1965). In other words, there are good grounds for believing that all varieties of the diagnostic process are at times subject to significant observer variation. But because of their specially vulnerable position, psychiatrists must be prepared to devote more attention than other diagnosticians to inter-observer differences and other variations inherent in the diagnostic process.

Influenced no doubt by these diagnostic discrepancies, authors such as Masserman and Carmichael (1938), Colley (1960), and Menninger (1963) have gone so far as to suggest that conventional descriptive diagnoses are so unreliable that they are best disregarded. Such pessimism is not justified, because the diagnosticians in the studies described above, and in virtually all the others in the literature, were working under ordinary clinical conditions. They had not undergone any special training, and at the most had only a brief acquaintance with an agreed rating-scale or with a glossary of terms. At least one study performed even under these minimal conditions of standardization achieved diagnostic consistency, probably because the diagnosticians involved had all had a similar psychiatric training. The study, by Wilson and Meyer (1962), stands in interesting contrast to that of Pasa-manick, Dinitz, and Lefton (1959) already noted. The distributions of differ-ent diagnoses in a psychiatric liaison service in a general hospital for 2 consecutive years were compared and found to be very similar, in spite of a different set of patients and a different set of diagnosticians. For instance, the proportion of patients diagnosed as schizophrenic remained at 15 per cent, all types of depression together changed only from 23 per cent to 26 per cent, and personality disorders changed from 38 per cent to 34 per cent (the number of patients dealt with was 128 and 166 in the 2 years).

Much more convincing evidence of the reliability of the diagnostic process, however, is available from specially designed studies, as opposed to those carried out under ordinary clinical conditions. One of the early reports on the development and use of the 'Present State Examination' (PSE) which was used in a modified form in the present study, demonstrated that a high degree of reliability can be achieved when diagnoses are made under optimal condi-tions (Wing, Birley, Cooper, Graham, and Isaacs, 1967). During work pri-marily directed at establishing the inter-rater reliability of symptom scores, a provisional diagnosis was made by the pairs of interviewers independently at the end of each interview. Since the PSE is directed only at the symptoms experienced by the patient over the last month, this provisional diagnosis is not a definitive diagnosis, but it must bear a very close relationship to it in most patients. The interviewers had all been trained in the same institute and all used a set of instructions geared to the interview and specially prepared for the purpose of making this categorization. Over a series of 172 patients (about half of whom had schizophrenia, just under half some type of affective illness, and the remainder a variety of other disorders) there was complete agreement on primary diagnosis in 84 per cent, when they were tabulated into 11 cate-gories. There was partial disagreement in 7 per cent, and serious disagreement in only 9 per cent, a large proportion of the disagreements involving the notoriously difficult category of 'personality disorder', or distinctions between different subcategories of non-psychotic affective disorders.

This high level of agreement showed what could be expected with a special effort to control known sources of inter-observer variation. Together with the recent emergence of other reliable clinical methods of interviewing and rating (Spitzer, Fleiss, Burdock, and Hardesty, 1964) and with the development of other types of standardized rating instruments such as Lorr's IMPS (Lorr and Klett, 1967), these results at last raised the possibility of a more systematic examination of the diagnostic process in psychiatry. As already noted, it had become increasingly obvious to those concerned with psychiatric epidemiology and statistics in America and in Britain that the differences between some of the mental hospital admission rates were the single outward manifestation of several possible differences between patients, psychiatrists, or hospital and statistical services, all worthy of investigation. The use of these standardized procedures as a yardstick to set against the more variable diagnoses used in official hospital admission statistics was an obvious and practical way of starting work in this field.

THE AIMS OF THE UNITED STATES–UNITED KINGDOM DIAGNOSTIC PROJECT

Against this background the United States–United Kingdom Diagnostic Project was formed, with a field of interest as wide as the ramifications of the diagnostic process itself. Rather than merely encouraging co-operation between different centres or groups of workers, it was thought preferable to create a research group that would remain one organization, although necessarily working in two countries, and the all-important problem of uniformity of method was minimized by paying special attention to the thorough and joint training of the interviewers on both sides in the same standardized and reliable interviewing methods.

The programme of the Diagnostic Project was envisaged as having two main stages:

1. First, studies of the relationship between mental hospital admission statistics and diagnosis, since this was one of the original and outstanding problems that had stimulated the formation of the project. Using standardized methods of assessment and diagnosis as a yardstick to set against hospital admission statistics, these studies would demonstrate the extent to which diagnostic variations between psychiatrists contributed towards the differences in hospital statistics, particularly with regard to manic-depressive psychosis and schizophrenia. Further development and improvement of the comparatively novel standardized methods of assessment would take place as a result of this type of study.
2. It would then be possible to carry out a more difficult but more important set of studies aimed at establishing the prevalence of mental disorders in various sociocultural groups in the two countries.

Concurrently with both 1 and 2, complementary studies using videotapes of psychiatric interviews were planned, in which audiences of British and American psychiatrists would make ratings and diagnoses as a means of investigating in more detail the sources of inter-observer variation in the diagnostic process.

As a necessary corollary to all these field studies, it was also envisaged that special attention would be given to methods of data analysis, particularly to the use of clustering techniques and factor analysis in relation to both the testing of conventional clinical ideas, and the development of fresh symptom clusters and syndromes.

In short, the study described in this monograph is the first stage in a programme aimed eventually at the investigation of the sociocultural correlates of psychiatric disorder. Part 2 (CHAPTERS III to XII) describes the Brooklyn–Netherne comparison, in which one hospital was studied on each side. Part 3 (CHAPTERS XIII to XVII) deals with the subsequent sampling study, covering the whole of metropolitan New York and London, for which nine hospitals in each city were used.

PART 2. THE BROOKLYN–NETHERNE COMPARISON

CHAPTER III

OUTLINE OF AIMS AND METHOD

THE aim of this investigation was to study a series of admissions to one psychiatric hospital in the United States and one in the United Kingdom, in such a way as to determine the relative contributions of:

1. Differences in the clinical states of the patients,
2. Differences in the diagnostic practices of the hospital psychiatrists,

towards the differences between the two sets of official diagnoses arising from the admissions.

Details of the design and methods used are described in CHAPTERS IV to VII but some of the major features of the design of the study may conveniently be commented upon here.

1. A hospital setting was chosen so as to allow direct study of the diagnostic returns which go through the routine channels to form the official admission statistics. The design was also such that it did not interfere with the ordinary working conditions of the hospital psychiatrists. Use of an area psychiatric hospital in England and a State hospital in the United States had additional value in that the results would reflect the working methods of members of the largest group of psychiatrists in each country who between them are responsible for the bulk of patient care. Other methods of studying diagnostic disagreement, such as obtaining diagnoses upon films or case reports, could have been used, but all these introduce distortions and limitations into the results.

2. For the results to be directly referable to the official statistics it was necessary for the study to be based upon consecutive admissions, including all that contributed to the official returns, however defined. In practice, this meant the same on both sides—a consecutive series of first and readmissions.

3. The hospital diagnoses were compared with independent diagnoses made at the same time on the same patients by the staff of the Diagnostic Project, using a set of interviewing, rating, and diagnostic procedures of known reliability, used consistently between the two sides of the project.

4. London and New York were chosen as suitable centres for the study, partly for geographical convenience and partly because each contains a large and important population of patients, psychiatrists, and hospitals.

5. The two hospitals selected were Brooklyn State Hospital in New York and Netherne Hospital in London. It was necessary to confine the study to one hospital in each city since the comparatively novel and lengthy standardized interviewing and diagnostic procedures had not been used previously on a large scale in busy hospitals, and it seemed unwise to launch straight into an elaborate study involving several hospitals. These particular two hospitals were chosen because their admission statistics were fairly typical (of England and Wales in the case of Netherne, and of New York State in the case of Brooklyn), as well as for practical reasons. This made it unlikely that the results would merely reflect local idiosyncrasies.

6. From the start, this study conformed to the basic principle of the Diagnostic Project, in that it was designed to be carried out by two halves of a single team, rather than merely being a co-operative study between two similar groups. Translated into practical terms this meant that to a large extent the interviewing personnel were interchangeable, both within each side and between sides. This interchangeability ensured that a good deal of very convenient flexibility was inherent in day-to-day working, once a satisfactory degree of reliability had been achieved in the use of standardized procedures for interviewing, rating, and diagnosis. As discussed later, the project psychiatrists were continually involved in joint interviewing and discussion of ratings and diagnoses, partly during the course of formal studies of the reliability and repeatability of the interviews, and partly because it was regarded as necessary for the maintenance of a high standard of comparability between the two sides.

CHAPTER IV

THE CHOICE OF PATIENTS AND HOSPITALS

THE differences between the admission rates of the United States and Great Britain for manic-depressive psychosis and schizophrenia were chosen as the object of study because they have been large, consistent, and well known for many years. These differences led Slater to suggest as long ago as 1935 (Slater, 1935) that a low incidence of schizophrenia in England might underlie the disparity, in spite of all the well-known problems of selection and differences in psychiatric facilities and possible differences in diagnostic criteria. Lewis commented in 1946 upon even larger differences between the figures for the first-admission rates for persons over 65 years for New York and England and Wales (Lewis, 1946), but was more cautious about drawing conclusions, emphasizing the important role that could be played by loosely applied diagnostic criteria. When emphasizing again the apparent excess of schizophrenia in American compared to British hospitals a few years later, Shepherd (1957) was also inclined to emphasize the possible contribution of diagnostic variation. The most direct and recent statistical comparisons were made by Kramer, and his figures constituted some of the original stimuli which gave rise to the present investigation. Kramer first presented his comparisons between the United States and Britain in 1961 (Kramer, 1961) and resummarized them with additions in 1969 (Kramer, 1969a). In TABLE I enough of his figures are reproduced to illustrate the size and nature of the differences. In spite of the closely similar rate for all disorders together, the individual categories show large orders of difference. For instance, the England and Wales/United States ratio for 'manic-depressive reaction' is 10·8 : 1 and for 'cerebral arteriosclerosis' it is 0·2 : 1. For certain age- and sex-groups, even more remarkable differences can be found, although the numbers become smaller, the most extreme example being for 'manic-depressive reaction' in the age-group 55–64 years, where both female and male rates in England and Wales are about 20 times their corresponding American rates. These differences are so large that middle-aged patients were chosen as having first priority for inclusion in this study. It seemed likely that the differences would turn out to be due partly to the patients and partly to the diagnosticians, so allowing both sources of variation to be examined. In fact, the whole adult age range from 20 to 59 years was finally included, so covering both the middle-aged patients expected to give rise to the greatest differences for manic-depressive psychosis, and the younger adults expected to give rise to the greatest differences for schizophrenia. The age range was restricted to those above 20 years and below 59 years as it was anticipated that patients

TABLE 1

FIRST ADMISSION RATES BY DIAGNOSIS, MENTAL HOSPITALS,
FOR THE UNITED STATES AND ENGLAND AND WALES, 1960
(*Taken from Kramer*, 1969)

| | AGE-ADJUSTED[1] RATES PER 100,000 POPULATION | | |
DIAGNOSTIC CATEGORY	*USA*[2]	*England and Wales*[2]	*Ratio: England and Wales/ USA*
All disorders	102·1	115·7	1·1
Schizophrenia	24·7	17·4	0·7
Major affective disorders	11·0	38·5	3·5
Manic-depressive reaction	3·3	35·7	10·8
Psychotic depressive reaction	2·9	DNU	NA
Involutional psychotic reaction	4·8	2·8	0·6
Diseases of senium	16·4	12·9	0·8
Cerebral arteriosclerotic psychosis	10·9	1·8	0·2
Senile psychosis	5·4	11·1	2·1
Psychoneurosis	12·4	22·9	1·8
Psychoneurotic depressive reaction	NA	9·1	NA
Other psychoneurosis	NA	13·8	NA
All other disorders	37·7	24·0	0·6

[1] Population of the United States in 1950 used as standard.
[2] United States: public and private mental hospitals combined; England and Wales: all mental hospitals.
DNU = Diagnosis not used
NA = Not available

within these limits would be more co-operative and easier to interview than either young or older patients. This was felt to be important since the necessarily extensive interviewing procedures had only been tried out under comparatively controlled and favourable conditions before this study started.

THE CHOICE OF HOSPITALS

For the same reasons, as adumbrated in the previous chapter, it was decided to limit the study to one hospital in London and one in New York in the first instance. For the United Kingdom, the 1965 admission figures for mental hospitals were obtained from the Ministry of Health, and a shortlist drawn up of those hospitals within reasonable reach of London whose figures were close to the average for England and Wales. These hospitals were visited, and the final choice of Netherne Hospital was made on practical grounds of facilities and co-operation offered as well as upon statistical criteria (TABLE 2 gives the admission data by diagnosis upon which the selection of Netherne was based).

TABLE 2

ALL ADMISSIONS, BY DIAGNOSIS, TO ALL MENTAL HOSPITALS IN ENGLAND AND WALES, AND TO NETHERNE HOSPITAL, 1965. PERCENTAGE TABLE[1]

	ALL HOSPITALS %	NETHERNE %
Schizophrenia and paranoid disorders	22·1	24·4
All depressive psychoses[2]	36·8	35·7
Senile disorders	8·0	12·3
Alcoholic psychoses	0·3	0
Other psychoses	5·7	5·0
Neuroses	14·9	10·4
Addictive disorders (incl. alcoholism)	3·5	3·1
Mental deficiency	0·5	0
Personality and behaviour disorders	4·8	5·7
Other	3·4	3·3
	100	*100*
	(159, 118)	(1744)

[1] Figures supplied by Mental Health Section, Ministry of Health.
[2] Manic-depressive, endogenous depression, and involutional melancholia.

TABLE 3

ALL ADMISSIONS (FIRST AND NON-FIRST) TO ALL NEW YORK STATE PUBLIC HOSPITALS, AND FOR BROOKLYN STATE HOSPITAL, BY DIAGNOSIS, FOR 1965, AGED 20–59 YEARS. PERCENTAGE TABLE[1]

	ALL STATE HOSPITALS %	BROOKLYN %
Schizophrenia	54·3	63·9
Involutional psychosis	5·1	10·5
Manic-depressive psychosis	2·6	3·9
Other psychoses	6·5	8·2
Alcoholic	10·6	6·7
Senile disorders	1·1	0·4
Neuroses	10·3	5·1
Other	18·4	1·2
	100	*100*
	($n = 22,211$)	($n = 742$)
Schizophrenia/all psychoses	0·76	0·74
Schizophrenia/manic-depressive	17·42	16·35

[1] Figures supplied by New York State Department of Mental Hygiene, Albany.

The same procedure could not be followed precisely in the United States because of a lack of comparable national statistics. However, the statistics for the whole of New York State were available, and these were studied in the same way. The final choice of Brooklyn State Hospital was again made partly for practical reasons: its admission figures are not the closest to the average for the whole of New York State, but they are not markedly different, and the ratios of diagnoses of schizophrenia to all other functional psychoses and to manic-depressive psychosis are very close to those for the whole of New York State [see TABLE 3]. (The eventual comparison of the data from Brooklyn and Netherne with the hospital sampling data described in Part 3 shows in fact that both hospitals reflected their respective samples to a surprising degree.)

CHAPTER V

THE CHOICE OF INTERVIEWING METHODS

THE MENTAL STATE INTERVIEW

IT is fundamental to the design of this whole study that diagnoses should be assigned to patients in exactly the same way on both sides of the Atlantic. In order to ensure this, it is necessary to do much more than simply to use the same diagnostic criteria on both sides. The clinical data from which the diagnosis is derived must also be comparable on the two sides, and they will only be so if the sources of information, the areas of inquiry and the methods used to elicit information are all the same. It is relatively easy to stipulate which sources of information should be used and which areas of inquiry should be covered, but far harder to ensure that information is always elicited in the same ways. It is well known that psychiatrists have very variable interviewing styles and that these differences may have a considerable influence on the information elicited. There is also evidence that, in the traditional unstructured interview situation, the expectations which the interviewer derives from his training and orientation influence his perception of symptomatology (Grinker, Miller, Sabshin, Nunn, and Munnally, 1961; Kendell, 1968). Abnormalities whose presence is anticipated tend to be sought more diligently and detected more readily than others, whereas those which are unexpected are liable to be glossed over, or not to be recognized at all.

The recognition of these shortcomings of ordinary clinical assessment has led in recent years to the development of 'structured interviews' which prescribe not only, as rating-scales do, the manner in which psychopathology is recorded, but also the way in which it is elicited. The questions the patient is asked, and their order, are both laid down in advance and ratings are made serially as the interview progresses rather than all together at the end.

Because of the overriding importance of maintaining a uniform procedure in both countries it was decided at the outset that all data would have to be obtained by standardized methods. This decision was basic to the design and execution of this entire series of studies. Two alternative structured interviews were considered for the assessment of the patient's mental state: the Mental Status Schedule (MSS) developed by Spitzer and his colleagues (Spitzer, Fleiss, Burdock, and Hardesty, 1964) at the New York State Psychiatric Institute and the Seventh Edition of the Present State Examination (PSE) developed by Wing at the Maudsley Hospital (Wing, Birley, Cooper, Graham, and Isaacs, 1967; Wing, Cooper, and Sartorius, 1972). The Mental Status Schedule is designed to elicit and record the symptoms experienced by the patient during the preceding 7 days, and consists of a booklet containing an interview schedule and a matching inventory of 248 dichotomous items. It is more highly standardized than the PSE; the schedule stipulates the exact form of words to be used for each question, and the corresponding rating or ratings are in most instances closely tied to the patient's reply. A small section of the schedule is reproduced below to illustrate this. Further probing is allowed if the patient's reply is incomplete or ambiguous, but only to a limited extent, by means of general queries such as 'Can you tell me more about that?', or 'What do you mean by that?'

What kinds of things do you worry about? (How much do you worry?)	4. Says he has felt elated or 'high'.	True/False
	5. Says he feels nothing, has no feelings, or feels dead.	True/False
	6. Says he has no worries or that nothing bothers him.	True/False
	7. Mentions he worries a lot or that he can't stop worrying.	True/False
What kinds of fears do you have?	8. Admits to three or more different fears or says that he keeps feeling afraid of different things.	True/False
	9. Mentions a fear of being abandoned or left all alone.	True/False
	10. Indicates he is fearful of losing his mind or losing control of his emotions.	True/False
	11. Indicates a morbid fear that something terrible will happen to him.	True/False

A PORTION OF THE MENTAL STATUS SCHEDULE (AFTER SPITZER)

The Present State Examination is more comprehensive (particularly in the sections concerned with hallucinations, delusions, and abnormal speech and behaviour in the interview) and contains nearly twice as many items—480 compared with 248. It also covers a longer period—the previous 4 weeks rather than the previous 7 days. Suggested probes are provided for each item, and are normally used, but the rater is free to ask additional questions if he feels this is necessary, and the rating he finally makes represents *his* judgement whether or not the symptom in question is present, rather than the patient's initial reply to the original probe. Different areas of psychopathology are usually covered in a specified sequence, though again the order can be varied if occasion demands. The scoring system is also more involved than that of the MSS, with several alternative ratings for each item.

In the hands of trained raters the MSS is highly reliable and, because its procedural rules are fairly clear-cut, raters do not require prolonged training before they become proficient in its use. However, its rather scanty cover of psychotic symptoms and the limitations placed on probing and cross-examining make it a less suitable instrument for establishing a definitive diagnosis in individual patients, particularly if they are psychotic. The PSE, by allowing the interviewer to vary the form of words he uses and to question the patient in detail, makes it easier to establish the presence or absence of crucial symptoms, but in doing so it inevitably becomes less completely standardized, and so more difficult to use in a consistent manner. Because the establishment of a reliable diagnosis, with particular emphasis on the differentiation of schizophrenic and affective illnesses, was one of the principle aims of the interview the Seventh Edition of the PSE was eventually chosen as the main instrument for this study, but 197 items from the MSS were also included on the assumption that their reliability would probably be somewhat higher.

A full description of the PSE is provided in the instruction manual (Wing, Cooper, and Sartorius, 1972) so only an outline description need be given here. All items are scored on a four- to six-point scale which allows ambiguous replies and omitted items to be identified separately:

o = Symptom or sign definitely absent.

1, 2 or 3 = Symptom or sign definitely present (ratings 2 and 3 are not always provided; when they are they denote increasing degrees of frequency or severity).

8 = The patient's reply is consistently ambiguous or unintelligible; or he does not reply, even when the question is repeated.

9 = Question not asked, or not applicable.

For some items definitions are provided, usually in the form of coding instructions, e.g.:

	No	Yes		NR	NA
ITEM 10. Have you worried about your physical health? (Rate only a painful preoccupation with the possibility of a malfunction or disease which has not been diagnosed medically. Rate 9 if the patient probably *does* have the disease.)	o	1	2	8	9

	No	Yes		NR	NA

ITEM 110. Have you lost any weight during the
past 3 months? 0   1 2 3   8   9
    1 = some but not sure how much.
    2 = less than 10 lb.
    3 = more than 10 lb.

For most items, though, the content of the rating is implicit in the wording
of the probe, e.g.:

ITEM 111. Have you actually gained any
weight? 0   1   8   9

ITEM 112. Have you had any trouble sleeping
recently? 0   1   8   9

Extensive use is made in the interview of 'cut-off' sections, containing
questions which are not asked if the preceding more general questions
indicate that the patient does not have symptoms of this type. For example,
general probes about worrying are followed by a cut-off section containing
detailed questions about financial worries, worries about health, worries about
other members of the family, and so on; if the patient denies having any
worries these more specific questions are omitted. This procedure enables
what would otherwise be a very lengthy interview to be completed within an
acceptable period of time, between 40 minutes and 1 hour in most cases.
The 480 items in the interview are also grouped arbitrarily into 48 'sections'
of varying size, each concerned with a single more or less well-defined area
of psychopathology, like obsessional symptoms or ideas of reference, or with
a global clinical concept like insight. Although the main purpose of this
arrangement is to facilitate administration of the interview, 'section scores'
can be calculated by adding together the scores on the individual items
within each section, and used as a convenient measure of disturbance within
that area of psychopathology.

The 197 items from the MSS and the 480 items of the PSE were combined
in such a way that each section of the interview was introduced by one or
more MSS items and these then followed by a series of more detailed PSE
items [see FIG. 1]. This was done primarily to prevent the MSS ratings from
being contaminated by information from what for them would have been
illegal questions, but it also had the effect of producing a reasonably natural
sequence of questions. This combined interview took between 40 minutes
and $1\frac{1}{2}$ hours to administer, depending on the patient's coherence and fluency
and the extent of his symptoms. This was not much longer than the time
taken by the PSE alone.

When the combined PSE/MSS schedule was in its final form, the six
psychiatrists involved in the study spent several weeks learning to administer
it fluently and ensuring, in a long series of joint interviews and discussions of

recorded interviews, that they were all conducting the interview and interpreting its procedural rules in closely similar ways. The fact that one of the project psychiatrists (J. E. C.) had been involved in the development of the PSE from its inception, and the fact that three of the others had received

THOUGHT

HOW ARE YOU AT MAKING DECISIONS?
            Says he cannot make up his mind OR that
            he has difficulty in making decisions.................................45:1 0 1

HOW IS YOUR MIND WORKING?
            Mentions his thinking is impaired OR
            that he keeps losing his train of thought
            or that he can't concentrate...............................46:1 0 1

(HOW IS YOUR THINKING?)
            Complains of a slowing down in his thinking............................ 47:1 0 1

    Do you seem to be very slowed down
    in your thinking recently? Worse
    than usual?................................. 76:1 0 1 2 8 9
        (1= occasionally, or moderately
        2= almost constantly, or severely)

    Do you find your thoughts get muddled, so
    that you can't get them sorted out?..................... 77:1 0 1 2 8 9

    Do you find it difficult to bring yourself to make
    up your mind? Can you make decisions easily?
    (rate subjective experience)............................. 78:1 0 1 2 8 9

CUT OFF IF INDICATED, & PROCEED TO NEXT ✳ AT SLOW

    Do you find yourself brooding so much that you neglect
    your work (housework)?..16:2 0 1 2 8 9

    Do you ever find thoughts racing through your mind?..........17:2 0 1 2 8 9

    Is there anything or anybody that interferes
    with your thoughts? (What is that like?) (probe only).

✳ SLOW
        DO YOU FEEL SLOWED DOWN IN YOUR MOVEMENTS?
            Admits he feels a slowing down in
            voluntary movements...48:1 0 1

FIG. I. A fragment of the combined (PSE/MSS) mental state interview.

their psychiatric training at the Maudsley Hospital, and so already shared many of the same attitudes and interviewing techniques, made this process much simpler than it might have been; but even so this long period of preparation was essential, for the PSE does allow considerable scope to the interviewer's judgement and it was vital for this to be exercised in the same way by everyone. At the end of this training period all six raters were able to use the schedule comfortably and with adequate inter-rater reliability [see CHAPTER VIII].

THE HISTORY INTERVIEW

In normal clinical practice a diagnosis is made on the basis of an examination of the patient's current mental state, together with an anamnesis obtained either from the patient himself or from a relative, or both. It was our aim in this study to preserve normal clinical usage, so far as this was compatible with the need for standardization, and also to obtain at least as much relevant information as would be obtained during a traditional clinical assessment. Accordingly, it was decided that the initial mental state interview should be followed by a structured history interview, and that whenever possible a similar interview should also be held with a relative, or other close acquaintance of the patient, in order to obtain an adequate account of the development of the patient's illness and reliable information about his family background, his personality and the salient features of his life.

As no suitable instrument was already in existence a structured interview had to be designed specially for this investigation. It is not possible to standardize a history interview to the same extent as a mental state interview. The function of a history is to elicit, not a catalogue of the symptoms present at a particular moment in time, but an evolving story of the development both of the patient's illness and of his life. The narrative quality is fundamental. If attempts are made to reduce the interview to a series of answers to predetermined questions the element of continuity and the relationships between one event and another are lost. People's lives are too variable for every situation or sequence of events to be anticipated, or for the same questions to be appropriate in every case. But though it is not practicable to stipulate the order and wording of the questions the patient is asked, it is possible to lay down a series of firm general principles governing the conduct of the interview, and thereby achieve a useful measure of standardization.

The history interview for this study was designed in the light of these principles with two fairly distinct aims in view: to provide a body of ratings covering the most important aspects of personal, family, and psychiatric history on which different groups of patients could be compared; and to compel the interviewer to question the patient about all the relevant aspects of the development of his illness and his background before making his final diagnostic formulation. The interview contained 232 ratings and normally took 40 to 60 minutes to administer. Ninety of these 232 were concerned with the patient's parents and siblings and his relationship with them, 78 with his personal history (his childhood, education, sexual development, occupation, personality, physical health, etc.), 50 with the development of the present illness, and 14 with previous episodes of psychiatric disturbance. In addition, there was a checklist of 57 symptoms with separate entries for the present illness and previous episodes.

A similar basic notation was used to that of the mental state interview. That is, for most items 5 ratings were provided:

0 = No or absent.
1 = Item or trait present, but not prominent.
2 = Item or trait prominent.
8 = Not known (either because the informant did not know or because the question was not asked).
9 = Not applicable (e.g. section on marriage for bachelors).

Potentially ambiguous items were defined as clearly as possible and suggested probes were provided for most topics, designed so as to elicit information without inviting agreement or denial. For instance, the opening section, concerned with the patient's relationship with his parents and their personalities, started thus: 'Tell me about your father.' 'What sort of man was he?' 'What was he like to live with?' If the interviewer failed to get adequate information by general probes of this kind he was allowed to ask direct questions but, if this was done, positive ratings could only be made on the basis of a clear description of examples of the behaviour pattern or situation in question. For instance, if the patient was asked 'Were you ever frightened of him?', a positive rating could only be made on the basis of a convincing description of an actual situation and not simply on the basis of an affirmative answer. Although the interviewer normally asked questions in the order presented in the schedule he was free to vary the order if he wished. He was also free to omit questions about sexual behaviour and delinquency if there were indications that they might cause offence, and if it seemed unlikely that they would be of any relevance to the current problem.

The patient history and the relative history both contained the same items and were governed by the same procedural rules. In fact, a single schedule was provided for both. It was assumed that in most cases the patient would be interviewed first, which meant that the patient's replies, and the ratings made from them, would be available to whoever interviewed the relative. This was done deliberately to allow the interviewer to concentrate on areas in which the patient's account had been deficient or implausible and to check carefully whenever the two accounts conflicted. It meant, of course, that the two interviews were not independent, but it accorded with normal clinical practice. A final set of ratings was made by combining those derived from the separate patient and relative histories. No formal rules were provided for dealing with the disparities between the two. It was decided simply to give precedence to whichever seemed more likely to be correct, in the light of all available information.

When the schedule was in its final form those involved in its administration went through the same lengthy period of training that had been used for the mental state interview and for the same reasons: to ensure that everyone was sufficiently familiar with the schedule to administer it fluently, and that all were conducting the interview and interpreting its procedural rules in the same way, and to ensure that inter-rater agreement was high. Because the interview was less completely structured than the mental state interview, this aim was, inevitably, not fully realized, but even so an important measure of standardization was achieved.

CHAPTER VI

THE PROJECT DIAGNOSIS

As the main purpose of this study was to compare patients' diagnoses on the two sides of the Atlantic it was essential for the same nomenclature to be used in both countries. At the time clinical diagnoses in British mental hospitals were not, in practice, restricted to any particular nomenclature, though the returns of individual hospitals to the Ministry of Health were converted arbitrarily by the Ministry to the nomenclature of the Seventh Edition of the *International Classification of Diseases* (ICD 7). In New York the system was different; a nomenclature was provided but it was based on the 1942 revision of the American Medical Association's *Standard Classified Nomenclature of Disease* and differed in many respects both from the then current American Psychiatric Association classification (DSM I) and from the *International Classification of Diseases*.

In this situation a decision was made to use in both countries the nomenclature of the new (Eighth) edition of the *International Classification of Diseases* for all diagnoses made by the project staff (referred to throughout this monograph as 'project diagnoses'). There were several reasons for this choice. The Eighth Edition had fewer defects than its predecessor and, because the American Psychiatric Association had decided to base the new edition of its own *Diagnostic and Statistical Manual* (DSM II) on ICD 8, we knew that it would shortly be coming into widespread use in both the United Kingdom and the United States. Even more important, there was a glossary available defining the meaning of the various categories recognized in the nomenclature. There are now two such glossaries, one British (General Register Office, 1968) and one American (American Psychiatric Association, 1968) which differ in a number of ways, but at the time the former was the only one available to us and so was used throughout the study.

This glossary was used as a reference standard to which the project psychiatrists were required to subordinate their personal diagnostic habits and preferences. This policy had two important consequences. It meant that the project psychiatrists used the full range of diagnostic categories listed in the glossary, whether or not they recognized them in ordinary clinical practice. A patient, for instance, developing a severe depressive illness for the first time after bereavement would be required by the glossary to be diagnosed as having a reactive depressive psychosis (ICD 298·0), whether or not the psychiatrist concerned was accustomed to using this term or whether he recognized reactive psychosis as a valid entity. It also meant that the glossary was always referred to whenever a differential diagnosis was under discussion and its descriptions used as binding criteria whenever they were sufficiently explicit for this to be possible.

The psychiatrist who administered the mental state interview made a provisional diagnosis immediately after this interview, and then replaced this by a final diagnosis after the history interviews with both patient and relative had been completed, doing so in consultation with anyone else who had been involved in the interviewing of that patient. In fact, however, this 'final' diagnosis remained open to revision because eventually every diagnosis was reviewed by a panel of three psychiatrists consisting of the interviewer, one of his colleagues, and, in the majority of cases, a representative of the other team (New York, or London, as the case might be). By this means, if the other two members of the panel disagreed with him, the interviewer's 'final' diagnosis could be, and sometimes was, changed.

Provision was also made for an alternative diagnosis if a second diagnosis was felt to be a serious possibility on the basis of the available evidence. A patient might, for example, be given a main diagnosis of personality disorder, schizoid type (ICD 301·2) and an alternative diagnosis of schizophrenia, latent type (ICD 295·5).

In fact, even after all three interviews had been completed, 35 per cent of the Netherne patients and 44 per cent of the Brooklyn patients still had alternative diagnoses. Provision was also made for one or even two subsidiary diagnoses if the patient had significant psychiatric abnormalities which were not covered by the main diagnosis. A patient with a main diagnosis of schizophrenia, simple type (ICD 295·0) might, for instance, require a subsidiary diagnosis of homosexuality (ICD 302·0) or alcohol addiction (ICD 303·2). In the event, 42 per cent of the Brooklyn patients and 31 per cent of the Netherne patients received subsidiary diagnoses, most commonly of some form of personality disorder. The introduction of subsidiary diagnoses of this kind allows a more adequate description of many patients, but it does create a situation in which spurious differences might arise. One patient might, for instance, be given a main diagnosis of neurotic illness and a subsidiary diagnosis of personality disorder while someone else with identical symptoms was given the same diagnoses the other way round. Situations of this kind were regarded by Ward, Beck, Mendelson, Mock, and Erbaugh (1962) as one of the most important of all sources of diagnostic disagreement. To prevent, or at least to minimize, them an arbitrary set of rules was imposed. A ranking system of illness was introduced with organic psychoses in first place, functional psychoses second, addictive states third, neuroses fourth, and personality disorders last, and it was stipulated that the subsidiary diagnosis must always be of lower rank than the main diagnosis. Thus, for example, in the case of the patient referred to above with both a neurotic illness and a personality disorder the neurosis would automatically be the main diagnosis.

The project diagnoses, both provisional and final, were based solely on the information derived from the mental state and history interviews. The patients' hospital notes were never looked at, nor were patients discussed with the hospital staff. It was essential to make this stipulation to maintain standardization and to prevent the project and hospital diagnoses from influencing one another. If access to hospital notes had been allowed and these had been of higher quality at one hospital than the other, an important bias would have been introduced thereby. This ruling did, however, have the important disadvantage of depriving the project staff of access to the findings on physical examination and to all laboratory investigations and psychological test results. Because of this it was agreed in advance that, if a situation arose in which the hospital staff were subsequently found to have diagnosed an organic condition where the project staff had not done so, the hospital notes would be inspected and, if the hospital diagnosis was clearly established by laboratory data, the project diagnosis would be altered accordingly. In fact, such a situation never arose, but if, for example, a patient diagnosed as a schizophrenic by the project had been given a diagnosis of amphetamine psychosis by the hospital on the basis of urinary chromatographic findings, the project diagnosis would have been changed.

No direct, formal study of the inter-rater reliability of the diagnoses made by the project psychiatrists was carried out, largely because the most important comparison, between the London and New York teams, would have been difficult and costly to organize. However, reliability was measured indirectly in several ways [see CHAPTER IX] and whenever joint interviews were done for any reason independent diagnoses were made by both participants and then discussed, and this served to identify and reduce the occasional idiosyncratic interpretations that did emerge. (To illustrate the level of agreement obtained in this setting the original diagnoses made by the interviewer and the observer of the last series of these joint interviews are shown in TABLE 4.) More important, though, was an exchange of staff between the New York

TABLE 4

THE RELIABILITY OF THE PROJECT DIAGNOSIS. INDEPENDENT
DIAGNOSES MADE BY INTERVIEWER AND OBSERVER ON
11 PATIENTS AT THE END OF THE MENTAL STATE INTERVIEW

PATIENT		INTERVIEWER	OBSERVER
		J. E. C. (UK)	R. E. K. (UK)
English Male, age 30	M:	Phobic neurosis	Anxiety neurosis
	S:	—	Asthenic personality
	A:	Anxiety neurosis	Phobic neurosis
		T. F. (USA)	J. E. C. (UK)
English Female, age 34	M:	Residual schizophrenia	Residual schizophrenia
	S:	—	—
	A:	Paranoid schizophrenia	—

TABLE 4 (*cont.*)

PATIENT		INTERVIEWER	OBSERVER
English Female, age 22	M: S: A:	T. F. (USA) Depressive neurosis Hysterical personality Hysterical neurosis	R.E.K. (UK) Depressive neurosis Borderline intelligence —
English Female, age 26	M: S: A:	J. E. C. (UK) Phobic neurosis — Anxiety neurosis	R. E. K. (UK) Phobic neurosis Borderline intelligence —
English Female, age 31	M: S: A:	T. F. (USA) Depressive neurosis — —	J. E. C. (UK) Depressive neurosis — —
English Female, age 27	M: S: A:	R. E. K. (UK) Manic-depressive psychosis, depressive — —	J. E. C. (UK) Manic-depressive psychosis, depressive Anankastic personality —
English Female, age 27	M: S: A:	T. F. (USA) Phobic neurosis Asthenic personality Anxiety neurosis	R. E. K. (UK) Phobic neurosis — Depressive neurosis
American Male, age 48	M: S: A:	L. S. (USA) Alcohol addiction — —	R. E. K. (UK) Alcohol addiction — —
English Male, age 24	M: S: A:	L. S. (USA) Catatonic schizophrenia — Paranoid schizophrenia	R. E. K. (UK) Acute schizophrenic episode Schizo-affective psychosis
English Male, age 31	M: S: A:	R. E. K. (UK) Paranoid schizophrenia — —	L. S. (USA) Paranoid schizophrenia — —
English Female, age 28	M: S: A:	L. S. (USA) Manic-depressive psychosis, depressed — Anxiety neurosis	J. E. C. (UK) Anxiety neurosis — Manic-depressive psychosis, depressed

KEY: M = Main diagnosis
   S = Subsidiary diagnosis
   A = Alternative diagnosis

and London teams. By this means not only were the two teams kept in constant contact with one another but a substantial number of the American patients were interviewed and diagnosed by members of the London team, and a smaller number of English patients diagnosed by members of the New York team. It was also, of course, a considerable, though unplanned, advantage that four of the six project psychiatrists, two from each team, had been trained at the Maudsley Hospital and so started with similar diagnostic preconceptions.

CHAPTER VII

THE TWO HOSPITALS, THE PATIENTS, AND THE INTERVIEWING PROCEDURES

THE HOSPITALS

NETHERNE Hospital is one of the ring of mental hospitals built around London at the turn of the century. It is situated 17 miles south of the centre of the city, between Coulsdon and Reigate, in what used to be part of Surrey but is now the London Borough of Croydon. In 1967 it had 1860 beds and about 1500 admissions a year. At that time its catchment area consisted of parts of the London Boroughs of Merton and Sutton, the Surrey towns Epsom, Leatherhead, Reigate, and Caterham, and their surrounding rural areas. Although the hospital itself is in rural surroundings, most of its catchment area is suburban, with areas of light industry in Merton and Sutton. Much of the housing was developed in the 1920s and it is a fairly prosperous area with a low unemployment rate and 60 per cent of homes owner-occupied. A high proportion of the working population is employed in Central London and 32 per cent are in professional or managerial occupations (Social Classes I and II).

The Brooklyn State Hospital differs in many respects. It is a larger hospital with 2600 beds in 1966 and nearly 2000 admissions a year. Its catchment area is the southern half of Brooklyn, the largest of the five boroughs of New York, and the hospital is situated in rather drab urban surroundings in the midst of this area. The population is predominantly white and a high proportion consists of second- or third-generation Americans of Italian or Jewish stock. There are substantial black and Puerto Rican populations in Coney Island and Flatbush, but the 'ghetto' areas of Brownsville and Bedford-Stuyvesant fall within the catchment areas of other hospitals. There are also several middle-class and upper middle-class residential districts, but the greater part of the area consists of rather old apartment buildings and scattered areas of light industry. Taken as a whole it is probably fairly typical of New York except that the small but wealthy white Protestant section of the city's population is probably under-represented.

In addition to these social and economic differences between the two catchment areas, the hospitals themselves play rather different roles in the psychiatric services of their respective cities. The most obvious difference is that New York's State hospitals cater mainly for the lower half of the social scale because the wealthy, and many of the not so wealthy, prefer to be treated in private hospitals, at least in the early stages of their illnesses. In London, however, private hospitals are few and cater only for a tiny proportion of the population. Another important difference is that in New York it is uncommon for patients to be admitted directly to a State hospital. The majority are admitted initially to one of the receiving hospitals which act as filters, retaining those patients likely to need only brief hospitalization and passing on those with more serious or more chronic conditions a week or two later. A further, but in some ways compensatory, difference is the greater availability of psychiatric out-patient services in London. Thus, whereas in New York most patients entering State hospitals have been treated first in a receiving hospital (King's County Hospital in the case of Brooklyn patients), in London many patients have already been treated either at one of the hospital's own out-patient clinics or by their general practitioner. Finally, there are important differences between the two countries in the legal status of psychiatric patients and in public attitudes towards mental hospitals. The effect of these is to make patients less reluctant to be admitted to hospital in London, with the result that a higher proportion are admitted voluntarily and perhaps also at an earlier stage in their illness.

If the purpose of this investigation had been to compare the prevalence of different types of mental illness in the two cities the large ethnic and economic differences between the catchment areas of the two hospitals would have been a serious, even fatal, flaw in the design of the study. But we were not concerned here with prevalence, only with comparative diagnostic criteria. For this purpose it was desirable that the two hospitals should be diagnostically representative—that is, that the diagnostic distribution of their admissions should be close to their respective national averages—but it was quite immaterial whether or not their catchment areas were similar in their social and cultural characteristics. Indeed, even if an effort had been made to match the two catchment areas on social variables it would still not have been possible to draw any conclusions about comparative prevalence from the results, for all mental hospitals deal only with a fraction of the mental illness in their catchment areas, and, for the reasons described above, the roles played by London's mental hospitals and New York's State hospitals are not strictly analogous.

THE PATIENTS

A series of 250 admissions was seen at each hospital in order to be sure of having sufficient numbers for differences of practical importance to achieve statistical significance. For convenience the interviewing was done in two stages. The first stage involved a series of 145 patients between the ages of 35 and 59 and the second, some months later, a series of 105 patients aged 20–34. At Netherne the admission dates of the first series ran from 1 November 1966 to 1 February 1967, and those of the second series from 5 September 1967 to 8 January 1968 (with one 7-day break in October 1967). At Brooklyn, where the admission rate was much higher, the corresponding dates were

14 February to 20 April 1967 (with one 7-day break in March) for the first series, and 14 November 1967 to 20 February 1968 (with four breaks totalling 32 days) for the second series. For most purposes thereafter these two series were treated as a single sample of 250 patients covering the age range from 20 to 59. It should be noted, though, that because the interval between the admission dates of the first and last patients was longer for the two second series than it had been for the first (117 days for the second compared with 92 days for the first at Netherne; and 66 days for the second compared with 58 days for the first at Brooklyn), combining the two produces an excess of younger patients, particularly at Netherne. For our purposes, however, this is of little consequence and the procedure does serve to impose some degree of age-matching on the two populations. In fact, the average age of the Netherne patients was 38·4 years and that of the Brooklyn patients 38·6 years. The sex ratios of the two were also similar to one another: 112 (44·8 per cent) of the Netherne patients and 120 (48·0 per cent) of the Brooklyn patients were male, and the difference is statistically insignificant (chi-square = 0·39 and $p > 0.80$).

Some of the social and cultural characteristics of the two series are shown in TABLE 5. The Brooklyn population contains substantial Italian, Puerto Rican, and black elements, whereas the great majority of Netherne patients are of native British ancestry. Even at Brooklyn, though, less than 40 per cent belong to any identifiable minority and only 18 per cent are non-white. In fact, the biggest difference between the two populations is religious rather than ethnic. Eighty per cent of the Netherne patients are from a Protestant background but at Brooklyn, where 47 per cent are Catholic and 29 per cent Jewish, those with a Protestant background form only a small minority.

These ethnic and religious differences are reflections of well-known differences between London and the 'melting pot' of New York and, although they may be accentuated here by the low proportion of immigrants in the Netherne catchment area, would be encountered in any comparison of the two cities. The differences in social class, in marital and occupational status, and in domicile are less basic. The higher proportion of Netherne patients who are working full-time, who are married and living with their spouses, and who come from the professional or managerial classes is a reflection partly of the fact that Netherne's catchment area contains a higher proportion of middle-class suburban dwellings than Brooklyn's, and partly of the fact that few middle-class patients enter State hospitals in New York in any case. To some extent they would be found in any State hospital–area hospital comparison, though here they are accentuated by differences between the individual catchment areas. The educational differences, on the other hand, particularly the higher proportion of Brooklyn patients with a university or college education, are a reflection of national differences which still stand out in spite of the selective loss of middle-class patients from the Brooklyn series.

The overall impression that emerges is that the Netherne patients are a relatively stable homogeneous population, sharing a common ethnic and

TABLE 5

THE MAJOR SOCIAL AND CULTURAL CHARACTERISTICS OF THE
BROOKLYN AND NETHERNE PATIENTS

	BROOKLYN	NETHERNE	p
ETHNIC BACKGROUND			
Italian	37	I	0·00I
Irish	16	16	n.s.
Negro	26	4	0·00I
Puerto Rican	17	0	0·00I
Asian or African	I	5	n.s.
RELIGIOUS BACKGROUND			
Protestant	46	20I	0·00I
Catholic	118	38	0·00I
Jewish	73	I	0·00I
SOCIAL CLASS (Registrar General's Classification)			
I or II (Professional or Managerial)	19	53	0·00I
III (Clerical)	93	90	n.s.
IV (Skilled manual)	55	37	0·05
V (Unskilled manual)	61	64	n.s.
EDUCATION			
Left school before age of 15	53	96	0·00I
Left school at 15 or 16	81	102	n.s.
University (college) or other higher education	40	21	0·02
MARITAL STATUS			
Single	104	83	n.s.
Married	77	139	0·00I
Divorced or separated	54	26	0·00I
Widowed	10	2	0·05
OCCUPATIONAL STATUS			
Wage-earner (full-time)	41	88	0·00I
Wage-earner (part-time)	24	12	n.s.
Student	4	2	n.s.
Housewife	43	65	0·05
Unemployed	130	77	0·00I
DOMICILE			
With spouse	77	131	0·00I
With parents	65	41	0·02
With other relatives or friends	39	21	0·02
Alone	52	29	0·01
Hostel or vagrant	10	26	0·01

religious background, mostly married and living with their families, and with steady jobs. The Brooklyn patients, on the other hand, are more diverse ethnically and culturally, and a high proportion shows evidence of social instability or failure—they are divorced or separated, or unemployed, or living alone.

THE INTERVIEWING

The mental state interview was usually carried out within 24 hours, and always within 72 hours, of admission. Sometimes patients were seen before they had been examined by a member of the hospital medical staff and sometimes afterwards; in either case there was no communication between project and hospital staff. Occasionally, patients were too disturbed for the interview to be completed at this time. When this was so, the behavioural ratings were completed and the rest of the interview deferred until later. Every patient who was regarded as an admission by the hospital, and who would therefore figure in the hospital's admission statistics, was seen, even though this occasionally produced anomalous situations. On one occasion, for instance, a long-stay patient was counted as an admission because he was returning from an overnight stay in another hospital after dental treatment; and it was not uncommon for the same patient to figure in the series two or even three times because he was readmitted soon after being discharged. The only exceptions to this principle were 14 patients, seven at each hospital, who were lost to the two series through circumstances beyond our control. Most of these were lost because they discharged themselves, or absconded, before being interviewed by the project staff, but two Brooklyn patients were lost through a clerical error. Rather than retain these 14 in the series undiagnosed they were replaced. Some information about them is given in TABLE 6 and it can be seen that the same sorts of patients were lost at both hospitals; at both five of the seven were male, four were under 30 and three received hospital diagnoses of schizophrenia. A further problem was posed by 15 patients, 14 at Brooklyn and one at Netherne, who were unable to speak English. Most of these were Spanish-speaking Puerto Ricans but two were Italians (one at each hospital), one was Egyptian, and one a low-grade mental defective. These patients were all retained in the series and the Spanish- and Italian-speaking ones interviewed as well as possible with the aid of interpreters. Surprisingly, no patients were lost at either hospital through refusal to be interviewed, in spite of the fact that the interviewer always made it clear at the outset that he was not the psychiatrist responsible for their treatment. In some cases, though, particularly at Brooklyn, co-operation was grudging and incomplete.

The history interview was conducted after the mental state interview, as soon as the patient was judged to be well enough to give a coherent account of his illness and the events leading up to it. Sometimes this was the same day as the mental state interview, sometimes a week or more later. In nearly every case the same psychiatrist conducted both interviews.

The interview with a relative was usually carried out last, sometimes by the psychiatrist but more usually by a social scientist or psychiatric social worker who had been through the same training in the administration of the schedule as the other members of the project staff. A determined effort was

TABLE 6

THE SEVEN PATIENTS LOST TO THE NETHERNE
SERIES

SEX	AGE	HOSPITAL DIAGNOSIS
Male	57	Anxiety depression
Female	37	Depression, ? termination of pregnancy
Male	41	Psychosis with epilepsy
Male	29	Paranoid schizophrenia
Female	21	Subnormality, ? schizophrenia
Male	20	Alcoholism
Male	24	Schizophrenia

(All seven were lost through leaving hospital within 48 hours of admission.)

THE SEVEN PATIENTS LOST TO THE BROOKLYN
SERIES

SEX	AGE	HOSPITAL DIAGNOSIS
Male	35	Schizophrenia, paranoid type
Male	59	Involutional melancholia
Male	24	Alcoholic psychosis (deterioration)
Male	31	Psychosis with psychopathic personality
Female	29	Psychoneurosis (reactive depression)
Male	28	Schizophrenia (other types)
Female	25	Schizophrenia (other types)

(The first two were lost as the result of a clerical error: the other five through absconding before being interviewed.)

made in every case to contact a relative, or failing that a close friend, of the patient and to persuade them to be interviewed. By this means an informant was obtained for 223 (89 per cent) of the Brooklyn patients and 210 (84 per cent) of the Netherne patients. At Netherne over half of these informants had to be visited at home. At Brooklyn few home visits were carried out; instead, over a third of the interviews were conducted by telephone. Surprisingly, it appeared that just as much information was obtained in this way as in a normal face-to-face interview. (It is doubtful whether this would have been so at Netherne but in New York the telephone is ubiquitous and widely used, and tends to be accepted as a natural medium of communication for a wider range of purposes than in London.)

CHAPTER VIII

THE RELIABILITY OF THE INTERVIEWING METHODS

DURING the course of the interviewing of the first series of 145 patients at Netherne Hospital detailed studies were made of the reliability of the mental state and the history interviews. Three psychiatrists (Cooper, Kendell, and Sartorius) were involved. For the mental state reliability studies 37 patients were rated independently by two of the three, one conducting the interview and the other sitting in as an observer. Then, a few days later, 25 of the 37 were reinterviewed by the third psychiatrist. A similar procedure was followed for the history: 26 patients were rated independently by the interviewer and an observer, and all but one were later reinterviewed by the third psychiatrist. The three raters were allocated at random to the three roles (first interviewer, observer and second interviewer) so all combinations of the three were obtained, and the second interviewer was always kept in ignorance of his colleagues' earlier findings and opinions. Patients from the parent series of 145 consecutive admissions were allocated to the reliability studies whenever the admission rate was low enough for two raters to be spared. The reliability study patients were therefore not a random sample from those 145, but the choice was independent of the patients' own characteristics. Different patients were used for the mental state and history studies to prevent the burden of interviewing from becoming intolerable for them.

This design enabled two distinct comparisons to be made:

1. Between the ratings of the first interviewer and the observer of that interview.
2. Between the ratings of the first and second interviewers.

In the first, the observer comparison, both raters are presented with exactly the same sample of patient behaviour, both verbal and motor, and so disagreement can only be due to differences in their assessment of the patient's replies and behaviour, or to differences in what they notice or hear, or to clerical errors. In the second, the reinterview comparison, there are many more sources of variation. The two interviewers may not conduct their interviews in quite the same way, perhaps wording their questions rather differently or probing more deeply in different places and, for reasons which may depend on them or on the patient, they may establish different sorts of relationship with the patient. Moreover, the patient's clinical state or mood may change in the interval between the two interviews, and his feelings about being asked the same questions all over again add an important new element.

The observer comparison tends to give too rosy an impression of reliability, because all variation in the conduct of the interview is eliminated. On the other hand, the reinterview comparison may give a spuriously low index of reliability, because the patient's clinical state may change in the interim, and because a second interview necessarily creates a new and different situation.

For assessing the reliability of individual items, both in the mental state and in the history, weighted kappa was used as an index of concordance in preference to more familiar indices.[1] This was done for two reasons. First, because chance agreement, which varies widely with incidence, is specifically discounted, so allowing meaningful comparisons to be made between the kappa values for items of differing incidence. And secondly, because different weights can be assigned to different disagreements in such a way as to convey their relative importance. The most serious disagreement, between a rating of 0 and a rating of 1, was given a weight of 3; disagreement between 8 and 1, 2, or 3, or between 1 and 3, was given a weight of 2; and the comparatively trivial disagreements, between 1 and 2, between 2 and 3, and between 0 and 8, were given a weight of 1. Kappa and weighted kappa both have a value of $+1 \cdot 0$ if agreement is perfect, of zero if agreement is no better than chance, and a negative value if agreement is worse than chance.

The results of the mental state study, or rather those relating to the Present State Examination items, have already been reported in detail (Kendell, Everitt, Cooper, Sartorius, and David, 1968) and need only be summarized here. The mean kappa value for all PSE items was 0·73 for the observer comparison and 0·41, considerably lower, for the reinterview comparison. Individual items varied greatly, from 1·0 to less than zero. It is impracticable to list them here, but one important general finding did emerge. In the observer comparison a consistently lower kappa value was obtained for items describing the patient's behaviour in the interview than for those based on his replies to questions. The mean for the former was 0·49, compared with 0·76 for the latter, and the difference between the two is highly significant ($t = 4 \cdot 7$ and $p < 0 \cdot 001$). The most important reason for the comparatively low reliability of behavioural items is probably that they are global judgements based on behaviour throughout the interview, whereas the others are largely based on verbal behaviour at a single moment—the patient's reply to the appropriate question.

The mean kappa value for the 197 MSS items was 0·68 for the observer comparison and 0·50 for the reinterview comparison. The difference between the mean kappa values for the observer and reinterview comparisons is

[1] Kappa $= \dfrac{P_o - P_c}{1 - P_c}$ where P_o is the observed agreement and P_c the chance agreement.

Weighted Kappa (Kappa$_W$) $= 1 - \dfrac{\Sigma W_i P_{oi}}{\Sigma W_i P_{ci}}$ where W_i is the weighting assigned to a given pair of ratings, P_{oi} the observed proportion with that combination of ratings, and P_{ci} the chance proportion with that combination of ratings. For diagonal cells, representing identical ratings, $W_i = 0$ so that Kappa$_W = 1$ if agreement is perfect (from Cohen, 1968).

highly significant, both for the PSE and the MSS items; but the difference in kappa between PSE and MSS items is not significant in either comparison, a rather surprising finding in view of the considerable differences in the formal rules governing the two.

The grouping of the 480 PSE items into sections, each dealing with a more or less well-defined area of psychopathology, and the calculation of 'section

TABLE 7

RELIABILITY OF SECTION SCORES

(Product-moment correlations)

	INTERVIEWER *V.* OBSERVER	INTERVIEWER *V.* SECOND INTERVIEWER
Worry	0·83	0·73
Tension	0·93	0·67
General anxiety	0·93	0·59
Situational anxiety	0·58	0·67
Phobic avoidance	0·81	0·65
Autonomic symptoms	0·97	0·83
Slowed thinking	0·80	0·57
Retardation	0·85	0·64
Ideas of reference	0·86	0·31
Self-opinion	0·88	0·58
Depression of mood	0·84	0·71
Signs of depression	0·62	0·73
Somatic symptoms	0·85	0·65
Irritability	0·92	0·44
Elevation of mood	0·85	(–·05)
Obsessional symptoms	0·93	0·78
Interests	0·86	0·78
Concentration	0·94	0·64
Depersonalization	0·96	(0·04)
Perceptual disturbance	0·81	(–·02)
Memory	0·85	0·42
Insight	0·79	0·66
Abnormal motor behaviour	0·72	0·73

scores' by summing the scores on all the individual items in that section, have been referred to in CHAPTER V. The reliability of the first 23 of these section scores, which between them cover the main part of the interview and most of the commoner areas of psychopathology, was investigated by calculating the correlation coefficients between the scores of different raters. These correlations are shown in TABLE 7. The average correlation between the section scores of the first interviewer and his observer is 0·84, and the corresponding average for the reinterview comparison 0·55. The negligible correlations in the reinterview comparison for the depersonalization, elevation of mood and perceptual disturbance sections require some comment. Most of the 25 patients involved had scores of zero in these three sections and none had a high score in any of them. These particular correlations are thus based only on a few minor symptoms in three or four patients, and so are of doubtful significance.

It may be rather difficult for the reader to assess how good an inter-rater agreement is indicated by the kappa values obtained here, because few comparable studies are available. Kappa is still an unfamiliar index of concordance to most psychiatrists, but the product-moment correlation coefficient used as an index of section-score reliability is familiar enough, and the mean value of 0·84 obtained for the observer comparison compares favourably with the results of most other studies of the reliability of psychiatric interviews. The mean value of 0·55 obtained for the reinterview comparison is harder to assess, again largely because other workers have rarely reported comparisons of this type. It is clear, though, that a reinterview comparison will inevitably produce a lower concordance than an observer comparison.

The reliability of the history interview was assessed in the same way as the mental state interview but the interpretation of the results is more difficult, because for many items the difference between ratings of 0, 1, 2, and 3 is qualitative rather than quantitative, and the weights allocated to kappa therefore inappropriate. For those items where the weights were appropriate the mean value of kappa was 0·62 for the observer comparison and 0·41 for the reinterview comparison. For the remaining items the average percentage agreement between raters was 82 per cent for the observer comparison and 66 per cent for the reinterview comparison. These figures indicate that the reliability of the history ratings is comparable to that of the mental state ratings, but too much should not be read into them. For one thing the variance of kappa was much higher for the history items, because the items themselves are more variable, ranging from relatively factual ones, such as whether or not the patient was seen by a psychiatrist before admission to hospital, to much less tangible judgements about personality traits before the onset of illness. Another problem, not encountered in the mental state, is the mutual dependence of different items. For instance, the decision about the date of onset of 'present illness' is often difficult or even arbitrary, and in consequence its reliability is low. But if two raters disagree markedly on this rating they will inevitably be prone to disagree about all the ratings referring to the period of the 'present illness'.

An important variable often left out of consideration in studies of interview reliability is the patient himself, whose coherence has a profound effect on inter-rater agreement. In this study there was a five- or sixfold difference in inter-rater agreement between the best and the worst patients. Psychotics gave rise to significantly more ($p < 0.001$) disagreement than non-psychotics and this difference was entirely due to the schizophrenics; other psychotics (mainly patients with severe depressions) were no worse than non-psychotics. Other variables like age, sex, and intelligence did not seem to be important.

Extensive studies, reported fully elsewhere (Kendell, Everitt, Cooper, Sartorius, and David, 1968), were made of the differences between the three raters. No important differences were found in spite of the fact that the third rater (a visitor to England who had received his psychiatric training in Yugoslavia) came from a very different background from the other two. One rater tended to rate higher than the others but a three-way analysis of section-score variance showed that none of the three had a detectable personal bias. There was, however, a suggestion in this analysis that the raters' styles might still have been influenced to some extent by their diagnostic impressions, in spite of the structuring of the interview.

CHAPTER IX

THE CONSISTENCY OF THE PROJECT DIAGNOSIS

THE measures taken to ensure that exactly the same diagnostic criteria were used in both countries have been described already—the use of a glossary as a reference standard, a common training period for both British and American raters, a review of London diagnoses by a panel containing a representative of the New York team and vice versa, and an interchange of raters between the two countries. Because so much hinged on the success of these measures it was necessary to check that they were effective. This was done in three different ways.

The simplest way was to examine the diagnoses made by the project psychiatrists when they crossed over between London and New York. Only

TABLE 8

THE PROJECT DIAGNOSES OF THE 145 PATIENTS IN THE
FIRST BROOKLYN SERIES, BY TEAM MEMBERSHIP OF
INTERVIEWER

DIAGNOSIS	NEW YORK TEAM		LONDON TEAM	
Mania	8	(8%)	2	(4%)
Depression	29	(30%)	14	(29%)
Schizophrenia	27	(28%)	16	(33%)
Neurosis or personality disorder	8	(8%)	5	(10%)
Alcoholism	16	(17%)	8	(16%)
Other diagnoses	8	(8%)	4	(8%)
TOTAL:	96		49	

chi-square $= 1 \cdot 248$ and $p > 0 \cdot 90$

nine of the Netherne patients were interviewed and diagnosed by members of the New York team, but 49 of the 145 patients in the first Brooklyn series were dealt with by members of the London team. Provided that patients were randomly allocated to members of both teams, and there is no reason to believe that this was not so, the diagnostic distribution of these 49 patients should be similar to that of the remaining 96 patients interviewed and diagnosed by the New York team, if both were using the same diagnostic criteria. The two distributions are shown in TABLE 8; they are very similar to one another and such differences as there are are statistically insignificant.

This is strong evidence that both teams were using the same diagnostic criteria but, strictly, it is applicable only to the 145 patients in the first

Brooklyn series. It is still possible that the two teams diverged later on while interviewing the second series of younger patients, or that the London team had previously used different criteria for diagnosing their own patients at Netherne. As only a small number of patients were involved in rater exchanges in the second series, other methods of checking diagnostic consistency were introduced.

The most important reason why consistency is so difficult to achieve is that in normal usage the relationship between individual items of psychopathology and the diagnosis is both complex and incompletely specified. The latter is derived from the former at least in part by intuitive means rather than by formal rules. It is, however, perfectly possible to elaborate a set of formal rules which will ensure that any given combination of symptoms will always generate the same diagnosis, and in recent years several computer programs with differing mathematical bases have been developed for this purpose. The application of such a program to the clinical ratings of the Netherne and Brooklyn patients would provide two sets of diagnoses which, though possibly inappropriate by ordinary clinical criteria, would carry a guarantee of absolute consistency from one patient to the next. Computer diagnoses of this kind have no more claim to be 'right' than any other sort of diagnosis, but they can be used as an arbitrary standard for checking the consistency of other diagnoses. For instance, if a computer diagnosed schizophrenia more frequently in the Brooklyn series than in the Netherne series one should expect, if the project criteria for this diagnosis were consistent, a similar preponderance at Brooklyn of project diagnoses of schizophrenia, and this should be so regardless of whether computer or project diagnoses of schizophrenia were commoner overall.

During the course of the study Spitzer and Endicott (1968) developed a computer program, Diagno I, for deriving a diagnosis from the scale scores of their Psychiatric Status Schedule (Spitzer, Endicott, Fleiss, and Cohen, 1970), an expanded version of the Mental Status Schedule. Diagno is based on a logical decision tree model which determines diagnoses in the same way that a flora determines the species of a plant. That is, it consists of a series of questions, each of which is answered 'True' or 'False', and the answer to each question rules out one or more diagnoses or groups of diagnoses and determines the next question asked. This program was used to generate a set of diagnoses for the 500 Brooklyn and Netherne patients from the 197 MSS items in the mental state interview. It was not ideal for the purpose, for two reasons. Diagno employs the nomenclature of the American Psychiatric Association's DSM I, which differs in several respects from ICD 8 on which the project diagnoses were based; and because the mental state interview did not contain all the PSS items needed for Diagno's input it was not capable of generating a full range of diagnoses. The categories most affected by this were alcoholism, personality disorder, drug addiction, and sexual deviation; for this reason comparisons between Diagno and the project diagnoses were limited to the two major categories of schizophrenia and affective illness. The concept of schizophrenia embodied in Diagno is considerably broader than that expressed in the project diagnoses, and the concept of affective illness correspondingly more restricted. For present purposes this is comparatively unimportant. What matters is that the Brooklyn/Netherne ratio should be the same, or nearly so, for the project diagnoses and Diagno. (In fact, this argument depends on an assumption that the proportion of different types of affective illness and schizophrenia is the same in both series of patients. This, of course, may not be so, but it is still probable that any major inconsistency in project criteria would be revealed by these ratios.)

The two sets of diagnoses and these ratios are shown in TABLE 9. The Diagno and project ratios are similar both for schizophrenia and affective

TABLE 9

PROJECT AND DIAGNO I DIAGNOSES FOR THE BROOKLYN AND
NETHERNE PATIENTS

| | BROOKLYN | | NETHERNE | |
	DIAGNO	PROJECT	DIAGNO	PROJECT
Schizophrenia (including paranoid states)	129	81	111	65
Affective illness (including depressive neuroses)	33	91	53	118
Other diagnoses	88	78	86	67

Schizophrenia
Diagno: Brooklyn/Netherne ratio = 1·16
Project: Brooklyn/Netherne ratio = 1·25

Affective Illness
Diagno: Brooklyn/Netherne ratio = 0·62
Project: Brooklyn/Netherne ratio = 0·77

illness, indicating that the project criteria for these diagnoses were the same in both hospitals; in so far as they do differ from one another they suggest that the project criteria were slightly broader at Brooklyn than at Netherne for both diagnoses.

A more elegant and sensitive way of checking the consistency of the criteria used to generate the project diagnoses is to carry out a canonical variate analysis (Rao, 1948), and then to compare the assignment of patients on the basis of their scores on the resulting variates with their project diagnoses. The simplest form of canonical variate analysis involves two populations, one with a clinical diagnosis of A, the other with a diagnosis of B (or not A), which have both been rated for the presence or absence of N items potentially relevant to the distinction between A and B. From these data the analysis produces a linear variate consisting of a set of weights for the N items which has the property of maximizing the ratio of between-group to within-group

TABLE 10

THE 50 ITEMS USED IN THE CANONICAL VARIATE ANALYSIS

1. Worrying (3a)
2. Tension headaches (3a)
3. Subjective anxiety (4a)
4. Panic attacks (4a)
5. Phobic (situational) anxiety (3a)
6. Lack of energy (3a)
7. Obsessional symptoms (4a)
8. Behavioural concomitants of anxiety (4b)
9. Abuse of alcohol or drugs (3c¹)
10. Obsessional personality traits (3c)
11. Depression worse in evenings (2a)
12. Difficulty getting off to sleep (2a)
13. Annoyed by trivia (2a)
14. Symptoms for over a year (2c)
15. Histrionic behaviour before admission (2c)
16. Suicidal attempt before admission (2c)
17. Sex
18. Age
19. Difficulty relaxing (3a)
20. Self-depreciation (3a)
21. Depression of mood (4a)
22. Frequent weeping (2a)
23. Loss of all pleasure in life (2a)
24. Depression worse in mornings (2a)
25. Loss of appetite (2a)
26. Insomnia (2a)
27. Inability to concentrate (2a)
28. Auditory hallucinations (2a)

29. Loss of insight (3a)
30. Behavioural concomitants of depression (3b)
31. Hears voices nearly every day (2a)
32. Subjective experience of disordered thought (2a¹)
33. Delusions of bodily control (2a¹)
34. Delusions of organized persecution (2a)
35. Delusions of guilt (3a¹)
36. Blunting of affect (3b)
37. Non-social speech (4b)
38. 'Schizophrenic' speech (4b¹)
39. 'Manic' speech (2b¹)
40. Impaired interpersonal relationships (2c)
41. Always prone to mood swings (3c¹)
42. Always nervous or highly strung (3c)
43. No friends (2c)
44. Major psychological stress in last 12 months (2c)
45. Recent increase in activity (2c)
46. Markedly suspicious recently (2c)
47. More outgoing and gregarious recently (2c)
48. Admitted because of violence or risk of violence (2c¹)
49. Previous episodes with full recovery (2c)
50. Total time in hospital previously (c)

KEY: 2 = Scored on a two-point (present/absent) scale
     3 = Scored on a three-point scale
     4 = Scored on a four-point scale
     a = PSE item from the mental state interview
     b = PSE item based on behaviour in the mental state interview
     c = Item from the history interview
¹ Composite item produced by combining two or more items from the original interview.

variance. So, when a score is calculated for each patient by adding together all his weighted item scores the distance between the mean scores of the two populations A and B is maximal. If three populations (A, B, and C) are included two canonical variates are generated; if four populations are included three variates are generated, and so on (provided the number of populations does not exceed the number of items). In the basic two-population case most A patients will obtain high scores on the variate and most B patients low scores, and the boundary between the two populations can be defined as the mid-point between their means. In theory there might be no overlap at all, but in practice, if unselected patient populations are used, there are nearly always a few B patients on the A side of the boundary and A patients on the B side, the number depending both on the ease with which A and B can be distinguished clinically and on the consistency of the diagnostic criteria employed. One could, however, arbitrarily rediagnose all B patients with scores on the A side of the boundary as A, and all A patients with scores on the B side of the boundary as B. In effect, this would replace the original clinical diagnoses with diagnoses based on a single consistent criterion, the score on the canonical variate. But the item weights of the canonical variate are themselves a reflection of the clinical criteria originally employed to identify the two populations A and B; so really what this arbitrary rediagnosis does is impose on every patient the pooled or averaged criteria employed by the raters responsible for the original clinical diagnoses.

Essentially, this is the procedure that was followed here, complicated only by the fact that three diagnostic groups were included—schizophrenia, affective psychosis, and neurosis. Every patient with a project main diagnosis in one of these categories (387 patients, 77 per cent of the total) was included and 50 items were used, 34 PSE items from the mental state and 16 history items [see TABLE 10]. These 50 were chosen for their relevance to the distinctions between the three diagnostic groupings in question in the light of the results of earlier analyses published elsewhere (Kendell and Gourlay, 1970a and b). The two canonical variates obtained are shown in TABLE 11, and FIGURE 2 [p.53] illustrates the way in which patients' scores on these variates determine their group membership. The mean scores on the variates of the schizophrenia, psychotic affective, and neurotic groups are identified by the symbols S, PA, and N. The line 'ax' is the locus of points equidistant between PA and N and can be taken as the boundary between this pair of populations. Similarly 'bx' is the boundary between the affective and schizophrenic populations and 'cx' the boundary between the neurotic and schizophrenic populations. Every patient is allocated to one of the three diagnostic categories by his position relative to these boundaries.

About 20 per cent of the 387 patients in the analysis received scores on these two variates which placed them in a different diagnostic grouping from their project diagnosis, but overall most of these changes tended to balance one another out [see TABLE 12]. At Brooklyn particularly the net effect was small; psychotic affectives increased from 67 to 68, neurotics increased from 35 to 36, and the schizophrenics were reduced from 81 to 79. At Netherne the changes were rather more substantial. Neurotics increased by 11 from 60 to 71, and there was a corresponding fall in the psychotic affectives from 79 to 72, and in the schizophrenics from 65 to 61. This implies that the project psychiatrists had been using a somewhat narrower concept of neurotic illness at Netherne than at Brooklyn, and a correspondingly broader concept of psychotic illness, particularly of affective psychosis. As over 60 per cent of both neurotic populations were depressives it is likely that the distinction between psychotic and neurotic depressions is the main cause of this discrepancy, the Netherne raters having a relatively greater tendency to allocate patients with mixed symptoms to one of the psychotic categories.

TABLE 11

THE WEIGHTS OF THE 50 ITEMS ON THE TWO CANONICAL
VARIATES

ITEM NUMBER	FIRST VARIATE	SECOND VARIATE	ITEM NUMBER	FIRST VARIATE	SECOND VARIATE
1.	0·18	−0·03	26.	−0·05	−0·16
2.	0·07	−0·05	27.	−0·26	−0·16
3.	0·08	0·13	28.	0·40	0·28
4.	0·03	−0·04	29.	0·16	0·19
5.	−0·05	−0·58	30.	−0·10	0·45
6.	−0·20	0·10	31.	1·11	−0·35
7.	−0·19	0·06	32.	0·78	−0·08
8.	−0·20	−0·01	33.	0·69	−0·26
9.	0·00	0·04	34.	1·40	−0·07
10.	−0·03	−0·04	35.	0·15	0·67
11.	−0·42	−0·12	36.	0·48	−0·16
12.	−0·22	−0·13	37.	0·64	−0·11
13.	0·10	−0·29	38.	0·23	0·18
14.	−0·03	−0·26	39.	−0·53	0·43
15.	−0·73	−0·41	40.	0·72	−0·08
16.	−0·27	−0·26	41.	−0·40	0·47
17.	−0·18	0·12	42.	−0·34	−0·01
18.	−0·13	0·17	43.	0·22	−0·32
19.	−0·07	−0·05	44.	−0·34	−0·16
20.	−0·03	0·21	45.	−0·61	0·36
21.	−0·16	0·11	46.	0·39	0·31
22.	−0·12	−0·18	47.	−0·69	1·12
23.	−0·16	−0·09	48.	0·65	−0·04
24.	0·04	0·62	49.	−0·33	0·12
25.	−0·64	0·04	50.	0·11	0·02

Mean Scores on the First Variate		*Mean Scores on the Second Variate*	
Schizophrenics	2·48	Schizophrenics	2·11
Psychotic Affectives	−0·86	Psychotic Affectives	2·79
Neurotics	−1·17	Neurotics	1·30

To summarize the results of all three measures of consistency: the diagnoses made by the project psychiatrists when they crossed over between London and New York suggested that the project criteria were identical in the two cities; the Diagno study suggested that the project criteria for schizophrenia and affective illness (psychotic and neurotic combined) were substantially the same in both cities, but possibly a little broader for both at Brooklyn than at

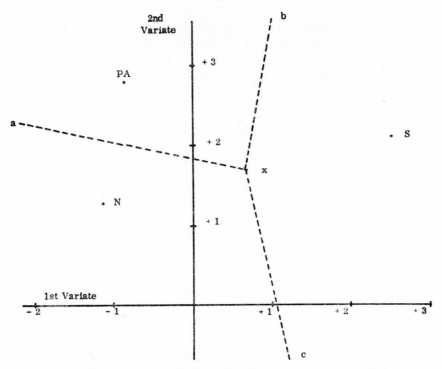

FIG. 2. The allocation of patients to diagnostic categories on the basis of their canonical variate scores. (See page 51 for an explanation of the symbols employed.)

TABLE 12

THE APPLICATION OF CRITERIA DERIVED FROM
CANONICAL VARIATE SCORES TO THE PROJECT DIAGNOSES OF
BROOKLYN AND NETHERNE PATIENTS

	A	B	C	D
Brooklyn schizophrenics	81	−12	+10	79
Brooklyn psychotic affectives	67	−17	+18	68
Brooklyn neurotics	35	−8	+9	36
TOTAL:	*183*	*−37*	*+37*	*183*
Netherne schizophrenics	65	−8	+4	61
Netherne psychotic affectives	79	−20	+13	72
Netherne neurotics	60	−11	+22	71
TOTAL:	*204*	*−39*	*+39*	*204*

A = Project diagnosis
B = Patients with scores on the two variates outside the appropriate range
C = Additional patients with scores on the variates within the appropriate range
D = Final total ('Canonical variate diagnosis')

Netherne; and the canonical variate analysis, the most sensitive of the three, suggested that the project criteria for neurotic illness were broader at Brooklyn than at Netherne, and the criteria for psychotic illness, particularly affective psychoses, correspondingly broader at Netherne. To some extent the implications of the Diagno and canonical variate comparisons are contradictory, which makes it difficult to draw confident conclusions from either. Perhaps the most appropriate judgement to pass on the combined results of the three studies is to conclude that they reveal no clear evidence of divergent criteria, but that they do indicate a need for a continuing surveillance of the project diagnostic criteria in future studies.

CHAPTER X

DIFFERENCES IN DIAGNOSIS BETWEEN THE TWO SERIES

SOME months after all interviewing had been completed the hospital diagnoses of the 500 patients in the study were obtained. This was done, not by examining the hospital notes, but by applying to the relevant statistical departments of the Ministry of Health in England, and the State Department of Mental Hygiene in New York. The reason for this somewhat round-about procedure was that the two sets of official statistics whose disparities had provoked this whole series of studies were derived from these sources, rather than from the hospitals themselves, and we were aware that, for a variety of reasons, the diagnoses originally recorded in the hospital notes and the eventual 'official' diagnoses were not always the same. For instance, in England and Wales, although hospital psychiatrists are asked to use the nomenclature of the *International Classification of Diseases* (ICD 7 at this time) this request is widely ignored and, in fact, a wide range of different terms and phrases are used by hospital psychiatrists and have to be converted, by a set of arbitrary rules, to the nomenclature of the *International Classification of Diseases* by Ministry of Health statisticians. To take one particularly important example, hospital diagnoses of 'depression' or 'depressive illness' are common and such diagnoses are coded by the Ministry as 'manic-depressive reaction, depressive type', a purely administrative decision which makes an important contribution to the apparent preponderance of manic-depressive illness in British mental hospitals. Similarly, a hospital diagnosis of 'probable schizophrenia' would be coded by the Ministry as 'schizophrenia, unspecified' whereas a hospital diagnosis of 'suspected schizophrenia' would be coded as 'diagnosis uncertain'. The hospital clerical officer responsible for the monthly returns to the Ministry may also exert a significant influence: one may conscientiously obtain full information on all patients while another, confronted with a set of clinical notes returned from the ward incomplete, may either copy an earlier diagnosis from a previous admission or simply record 'diagnosis uncertain'.

The official hospital diagnoses of the two series of patients cannot be compared in detail because the two are based on different nomenclatures—ICD 7 in the case of the Netherne patients, and the 1942 edition of the *Standard Classified Nomenclature of Disease* for the Brooklyn patients. Major categories like schizophrenia, manic-depressive illness, and neurosis are common to both, and so can be compared without difficulty. But they are subdivided in different ways in the two, and accompanied by other groupings which are only represented in one or the other. For this reason the two sets of 'hospital diagnoses' shown in TABLE 13 have been combined into 10 broad groupings. It is obvious from this table that the two distributions are very different from one another. Nearly two-thirds of the Brooklyn patients are schizophrenics, compared with only one-third of the Netherne patients. On the other hand, one-third of the Netherne series have depressive psychoses, compared with only 7 per cent of the Brooklyn series, a difference of more than fourfold. Similarly, there are four times as many neurotics (12 per cent v. 3 per cent)

TABLE 13

THE HOSPITAL DIAGNOSES OF THE BROOKLYN AND
NETHERNE PATIENTS

| | BROOKLYN | | NETHERNE | |
DIAGNOSIS	Total	%	Total	%
Schizophrenia	163	65·2	85	34·0**
Depressive psychoses	18	7·2	82	32·8**
Manic-depressive, manic	2	0·8	4	1·6
Depressive neuroses	6	2·4	10	4·0
Other neuroses	1	0·4	20	8·0**
Personality disorders	2	0·8	21	8·4**
Alcoholic disorders	31	12·4	11	4·4**
Drug dependence	3	1·2	5	2·0
Organic psychoses	7	2·8	5	2·0
Other diagnoses	17	6·8	7	2·8*
TOTAL:	250		250	

NOTE: Here, and in the following tables, ** indicates that the difference between the two percentages is statistically significant at the 1 per cent level (using critical ratios) and * that it is significant at the 5 per cent level.

and eight times as many patients with personality disorders (8 per cent v. 1 per cent) at Netherne as at Brooklyn, and three times as many alcoholics (12 per cent v. 4 per cent) at Brooklyn as at Netherne. In other words, the familiar differences between the two sets of national statistics have emerged again.

The two sets of project diagnoses, shown in TABLE 14, give a very different picture, however. Now only 32 per cent of the Brooklyn patients are diagnosed as schizophrenics and the difference between this and the 26 per cent of Netherne patients so diagnosed is not statistically significant. Nor are the four- and eightfold differences obtained for other diagnostic categories between the two sets of hospital diagnoses to be found. Affective illnesses are still significantly commoner in the Netherne than in the Brooklyn series, both overall and for manic-depressive depressions and depressive neuroses separately, but the differences are all less than twofold and there are actually more manic illnesses at Brooklyn than at Netherne. There are significantly

TABLE 14

THE 'PROJECT DIAGNOSES' OF THE BROOKLYN AND
NETHERNE PATIENTS

| | BROOKLYN | | NETHERNE | |
	Total	%	Total	%
SCHIZOPHRENIA AND PARANOID STATES				
Simple schizophrenia	7	2·8	3	1·2
Hebephrenic type	5	2·0	10	4·0
Catatonic type	5	2·0	3	1·2
Paranoid type	32	12·8	21	8·4
Acute schizophrenic episode	—		1	0·4
Latent schizophrenia	—		4	1·6
Residual schizophrenia	16	6·4	13	5·2
Schizo-affective type	11	4·4	6	2·4
Schizophrenia, unspecified	3	1·2	1	0·4
Paranoia	1	0·4	2	0·8
Involutional paraphrenia	1	0·4	1	0·4
TOTAL:	81	32·4	65	26·0
AFFECTIVE ILLNESS				
Involutional melancholia	—		5	2·0
MD psychosis, depressed	33	13·2	51	20·4*
Reactive depressive psychosis	7	2·8	8	3·2
Depressive neurosis	24	9·6	39	15·6*
MD psychosis, circular	5	2·0	5	2·0
MD psychosis, manic	17	6·8	9	3·6
Affective psychosis, unspecified	5	2·0	1	0·4
TOTAL:	91	36·4	118	47·2*
NEUROSES (other than depressive)				
Anxiety neurosis	3	1·2	11	4·4*
Hysterical neurosis	—		3	1·2
Phobic neurosis	2	0·8	3	1·2
Obsessional neurosis	3	1·2	2	0·8
Neurasthenia	2	0·8	1	0·4
Hypochondriacal neurosis	1	0·4	1	0·4
TOTAL:	11	4·4	21	8·4
PERSONALITY DISORDERS				
Paranoid type	—		2	0·8
Affective type	—		1	0·4
Explosive type	3	1·2	4	1·6
Hysterical type	1	0·4	1	0·4
Antisocial type	1	0·4	1	0·4
Others	1	0·4	2	0·8
TOTAL:	6	2·4	11	4·4

TABLE 14 (*cont.*)

	BROOKLYN		NETHERNE	
	Total	%	*Total*	%
ALCOHOLISM				
Excessive drinking	1	0·4	4	1·6
Alcoholic addiction	15	6·0	11	4·8
Delirium tremens	8	3·2	1	0·4*
Korsakoff's psychosis	2	0·8	—	
Other alcoholic hallucinosis	2	0·8	—	
Alcoholic paranoia	1	0·4	—	
TOTAL:	*29*	*11·6*	*16*	*6·4**
DRUG DEPENDENCE				
Opium derivatives	4	1·6	2	0·8
Barbiturates	2	0·8	3	1·2
Other drugs	2	0·8	2	0·8
TOTAL:	*8*	*3·2*	*7*	*2·8*
ORGANIC PSYCHOSES				
Presenile dementia	—		2	0·8
Psychosis with epilepsy	1	0·4	1	0·4
Psychosis with brain trauma	1	0·4	—	
Psychosis with intracranial neoplasm	1	0·4	—	
Psychosis with drug intoxication	3	1·2	1	0·4
Other organic psychoses	3	1·2	—	
TOTAL:	*9*	*3·6*	*4*	*1·6*
OTHER DIAGNOSES				
Mental retardation	4	1·6	1	0·4
Unspecified psychosis	2	0·8	—	
Transient situational disturbance	—		2	0·8
Sexual deviation	2	0·8	1	0·4
Non-psychotic disorder with convulsive disorder	4	1·6	1	0·4
Non-psychotic disorder with brain trauma	—		1	0·4
Acute paranoid reaction	1	0·4	—	
Tic	—		1	0·4
Non-psychotic disorder with other physical condition	1	0·4	—	
No psychiatric abnormality	1	0·4	1	0·4
TOTAL:	*15*	*6·0*	*8*	*3·2*

NOTE: Here and elsewhere depressive neuroses have been grouped with the affective psychoses, rather than with other types of neurosis. This has been done partly to facilitate discussion of the affective illnesses as a whole, and partly because of the considerable practical difficulties in distinguishing reliably between psychotic and neurotic depressions. For similar reasons paranoid states have been grouped with schizophrenia.

more anxiety neuroses at Netherne, but there is no longer any significant excess either of non-depressive neuroses as a whole, or of personality disorders. Only one diagnostic category—alcoholism—remains relatively unchanged; here there is still a significant excess at Brooklyn both of alcoholic disorders as a whole and of patients with delirium tremens. In short, replacement of the original hospital diagnoses by 'project' diagnoses has greatly reduced the differences between the two series of patients, and this is true for every major diagnostic category. But some significant differences still remain. Manic-depressive depressions, depressive neuroses, and anxiety neuroses are still commoner at Netherne, and alcoholic disorders still commoner at Brooklyn.

The measures taken to ensure that the project diagnosis was derived in consistent ways on the two sides of the Atlantic, and the success of these measures, have been described in the previous chapter. The fact that the disparity between the two sets of project diagnoses is much less than that between the two sets of hospital diagnoses suggests, therefore, that the differences between the hospital diagnoses are largely, but not entirely, due to differences in diagnostic usage on the two sides of the Atlantic, rather than to genuine differences in the patients. Even if the adjustments to the project diagnoses suggested by the results of the canonical variate analysis [see CHAPTER IX] are applied, this conclusion remains unaffected. Even with these alterations there is still no significant difference between the proportions of Brooklyn and Netherne patients diagnosed as schizophrenic, and while the difference between the numbers of neurotic patients at Netherne and Brooklyn is increased somewhat, that between the numbers of psychotic affectives is reduced even further.

It is clear from a comparison of TABLES 13 and 14 that there are substantial differences between the hospital and project diagnoses for both hospitals. The relationship between the two sets of diagnoses for the Brooklyn patients is shown in TABLE 15. Less than half those diagnosed as schizophrenics by the hospital staff are regarded as schizophrenic by the project psychiatrists, but, on the other hand, almost all those diagnosed as schizophrenics by the project psychiatrists receive the same diagnosis from the hospital. The biggest discrepancy is over the manic phase of manic-depressive illness. Only one of the 22 patients with a project diagnosis of mania has the same hospital diagnosis. Similar though less extreme discrepancies exist for depressive neuroses, other neuroses, and personality disorders. In fact, none of these categories is used with any frequency by the hospital staff, who regard the majority of those allocated by the project staff to any of these categories as schizophrenics. The closest agreement between the two sets of diagnoses is for alcoholic disorders. Here there is an 80 per cent agreement between the two, compared with 51 per cent agreement overall.

The analogous comparison for the Netherne patients is shown in TABLE 16. Only 54 of the 85 patients with hospital diagnoses of schizophrenia also have

TABLE 15

A COMPARISON BETWEEN THE HOSPITAL AND PROJECT DIAGNOSES OF THE BROOKLYN PATIENTS

HOSPITAL DIAGNOSIS	MAIN PROJECT DIAGNOSES										
	Schizo-phrenia	Dep. Psych.	Mania	Dep. Neur.	Other Neur.	Pers. Dis.	Alcoh. Dis.	Drug Dep.	Organ. Psych.	Other Dis.	TOTAL
Schizophrenia	76	29	20	13	7	5	2	2	7	2	163
Depressive psychoses	1	10	1	3	2	—	1	—	—	—	18
Mania	1	—	1	—	—	—	—	—	—	—	2
Depressive neuroses	—	2	—	3	—	1	—	—	—	—	6
Other neuroses	—	—	—	—	1	—	—	—	—	—	1
Personality disorders	—	—	—	—	—	1	1	—	—	—	2
Alcoholic disorders	—	3	—	2	—	—	24	—	—	2	31
Drug dependence	—	—	—	—	—	—	—	3	—	—	3
Organic psychoses	2	—	—	—	—	—	—	—	2	3	7
Other disorders	1	1	—	3	1	1	1	3	—	6	17
TOTAL:	81	45	22	24	11	8	29	8	9	13	250

TABLE 16

A COMPARISON BETWEEN THE HOSPITAL AND PROJECT DIAGNOSES OF THE NETHERNE PATIENTS

HOSPITAL DIAGNOSIS	MAIN PROJECT DIAGNOSES										
	Schizo-phrenia	Dep. Psych.	Mania	Dep. Neur.	Other Neur.	Pers. Dis.	Alcoh. Dis.	Drug Dep.	Organ. Psych.	Other Dis.	TOTAL
Schizophrenia	54	16	6	2	3	1	1	1	1	—	85
Depressive psychoses	3	40	2	22	3	4	2	3	—	3	82
Mania	—	—	3	—	—	—	1	—	—	—	4
Depressive neuroses	2	3	—	2	2	—	1	—	—	—	10
Other neuroses	2	2	—	6	9	—	1	—	—	—	20
Personality disorders	1	1	—	3	4	6	1	1	1	3	21
Alcoholic disorders	1	—	—	—	—	—	9	1	—	—	11
Drug dependence	2	—	—	1	—	1	—	1	—	—	5
Organic psychoses	—	1	2	1	—	—	—	—	1	—	5
Other disorders	—	2	1	2	—	—	—	—	1	1	7
TOTAL:	65	65	14	39	21	12	16	7	4	7	250

project diagnoses of schizophrenia. For depressive psychoses the corresponding proportion is even lower—40 out of 82—largely because over half of the remaining 42 were diagnosed as having depressive neuroses by the project psychiatrists. (Actually, a large number of these patients were simply given diagnoses of depression by the hospital psychiatrists, and these then coded as manic-depressive depression at the Ministry of Health.) As at Brooklyn, the hospital staff used the diagnoses of mania and depressive neurosis less frequently than the project staff but, unlike Brooklyn, they diagnosed other neuroses and personality disorders quite frequently. Overall there is 50 per cent agreement between hospital and project diagnoses, the same figure as at Brooklyn. As four of the six project psychiatrists had originally been trained in London, and so had inevitably been instilled with British diagnostic concepts, one would expect closer agreement between hospital and project diagnoses in London than in New York. There are two reasons why this did not occur. One is the spurious disagreement between psychotic and neurotic depressions referred to above; the other is that the psychiatric staff at Netherne tend to have a rather broader concept of schizophrenia than other London psychiatrists. At all events, other research teams have commented in the past (Parkes, 1963; Brown, Bone, Dalison, and Wing, 1966) that Netherne psychiatrists seemed to diagnose schizophrenia more readily than their colleagues in other mental hospitals, and such a tendency would explain why over a third of the patients in this series with hospital diagnoses of schizophrenia received other diagnoses from the project staff.

CHAPTER XI

SYMPTOM DIFFERENCES BETWEEN THE TWO SERIES

MEAN scores were calculated for the 250 patients from each hospital on each of the 48 sections of the mental state interview and the two groups then compared, section by section. The distribution of scores on each of the 480 PSE items and the 232 history items was also calculated for both groups and these also compared with one another, item by item. This was done for a variety of reasons. First, as a check on the consistency of the project diagnoses—to check, for example, that a preponderance of patients diagnosed as schizophrenic in one population was accompanied by a preponderance of schizophrenic symptoms. Secondly, in order to detect differences in symptoms transcending traditional diagnostic categories, and thirdly, to relate these symptom differences to some of the many social and economic differences between the two populations.

The results of the comparison between the PSE section scores of the Brooklyn and Netherne patients are shown in TABLE 17. The Netherne patients obtain significantly higher scores on most of the sections concerned with depressive symptoms—depression of mood, loss of self-esteem, loss of interests, slowed thinking, loss of concentration, retardation and subjective memory impairment—and this accords well with the predominance of patients diagnosed as having depressive illnesses. The Brooklyn patients, on the other hand, obtain higher scores on three sections which would be expected to predominate in schizophrenics—behavioural abnormalities, blunting of affect and incomprehensibility of speech—and this again accords with the higher proportion diagnosed as schizophrenics.

In spite of the standardization of the interview schedules and the efforts made by the London and New York raters to use them in the same way, one cannot be certain that all the section-score differences listed in TABLE 17 are entirely due to differences in the patients. They could, at least in part, be due to unrecognized differences between the two teams of raters. However, during the first (35–59 age-group) study, 49 of the 145 Brooklyn patients were interviewed by members of the London team and the existence of this substantial number of patients in one country rated by the other's psychiatrists makes it possible to test for the presence of rater differences. A comparison was made between the section scores of these 49 Brooklyn patients and those of the 142 Netherne patients who had been interviewed by the same three raters and it was argued that any Brooklyn–Netherne difference which emerged at a significant level in this comparison could confidently be attributed to the patients alone. Sections for which this was true are marked with a superior figure 1 in TABLE 17. (The converse, of course, is not true, if only because a comparison between groups of 49 and 142 will inevitably yield fewer significant differences than a comparison between two groups of 250.)

TABLE 17

ALL 250 BROOKLYN PATIENTS *V.* ALL 250 NETHERNE
PATIENTS. PSE SECTION SCORES

1. MEAN SECTION SCORES SIGNIFICANTLY HIGHER IN THE BROOKLYN
PATIENTS

| | MEAN SCORE | | |
	BROOKLYN	NETHERNE	*p*
Ambiguous replies[1]	7·06	2·56	0·001
Behavioural abnormalities[1]	0·30	0·08	0·001
Blunting of affect	1·05	0·52	0·01
Incomprehensibility of speech	1·06	0·56	0·01
Irritability	0·92	0·50	0·01

2. MEAN SECTION SCORES SIGNIFICANTLY HIGHER IN THE NETHERNE
PATIENTS

| | MEAN SCORE | | |
	NETHERNE	BROOKLYN	*p*
Depression of mood[1]	6·56	4·86	0·001
Loss of self-esteem[1]	3·01	2·26	0·001
Loss of interests	1·78	1·34	0·01
Slowed thinking[1]	4·04	3·04	0·01
Loss of concentration	1·83	1·38	0·01
Obsessional symptoms	0·81	0·49	0·05
Retardation[1]	2·10	1·69	0·05
Subjective memory impairment	1·17	0·92	0·05

NOTE: Here and elsewhere the significance levels of differences between mean
section scores are derived from *t* tests.

[1] A difference, significant at the 5 per cent level or beyond, was also found on this section in a comparison between 49 Brooklyn patients and 142 Netherne patients rated by London raters.

The high 'ambiguous replies' score obtained by the Brooklyn patients requires some comment, particularly as it seems to be a genuine patient difference. This section score is derived by adding together all the ratings of 8 (used whenever the rater persistently fails to get a clear reply from the patient) in the interview. Schizophrenics tend to give ambiguous replies more often than other patients and there are more schizophrenics in the Brooklyn series, but this predominance is not nearly enough to account for a disparity of this magnitude. Probably the most important cause is the relatively high proportion of the Brooklyn patients who were first-generation immigrants with an imperfect command of English. The difficulties produced by Spanish-speaking immigrants from Puerto Rico and Latin America have already been commented upon, and, in spite of the assistance of interpreters, this group was responsible for a high proportion of the ambiguous replies

TABLE 18A

ALL 250 BROOKLYN PATIENTS *V.* ALL 250 NETHERNE PATIENTS.
PSE ITEMS SIGNIFICANTLY COMMONER IN THE BROOKLYN PATIENTS

| | TOTAL NUMBER | | |
	BROOKLYN	NETHERNE	p
Loss of insight	90	58	0·01
Feeling of being accused by others	17	4	0·01
Constipation	68	43	0·01
Financial worries	82	61	0·05
Bothered by a particular person	93	70	0·05
Weight gain in last 3 months	56	35	0·05
Feeling of something strange going on	54	34	0·05
Things look grey or colourless	8	1	0·05
Delusions about bodily appearance	11	2	0·05
BEHAVIOURAL RATINGS:			
Finger tremor	103	48	0·001
Unkempt appearance	20	3	0·001
Dysplastic body build	11	1	0·01
Blunting of affect—overall rating	51	24	0·01
Expressionless face	40	16	0·01
Very rapid speech	15	3	0·01
Complete apathy	16	4	0·02
Little spontaneous speech	29	12	0·05
Idiosyncratic usage of ordinary words	9	1	0·05
Vague wandering of theme of speech	10	2	0·05

NOTE: Totals given here are for ratings of 1 and 2 combined.
    The significance levels quoted are derived from chi-square tests.

ratings. However, it is possible that the fact that none of the New York raters was a native of the city, or even a native-born American, also contributed to the greater communication difficulties at Brooklyn.

TABLE 18A lists those PSE items which were found to be significantly commoner in the Brooklyn patients and TABLE 18B those which were commoner in the Netherne patients. (A few items have been omitted, but only because their content was very similar to that of others which are included.) The general pattern confirms and amplifies the section-score differences. More symptoms predominate in the Netherne patients than in the Brooklyn patients and almost all are typical features of depressive illnesses. The only

TABLE 18B

ALL 250 BROOKLYN PATIENTS *V*. ALL 250 NETHERNE PATIENTS. PSE
ITEMS SIGNIFICANTLY COMMONER IN THE NETHERNE PATIENTS

| | TOTAL NUMBER | | |
	NETHERNE	BROOKLYN	*p*
Severe or constant worrying	84	48	0·001
Situational anxiety—overall rating	78	46	0·001
Phobic avoidance—overall rating	74	38	0·001
Loss of self-confidence	122	71	0·001
Feeling that life is not worth living	134	72	0·001
Suicidal thoughts or attempts	114	66	0·001
Loss of appetite	131	84	0·001
Sleeping tablets before admission	123	73	0·001
Neglect of personal appearance	89	49	0·001
Inability to concentrate	141	91	0·001
Subjective memory disturbance	117	69	0·001
Muddled thinking	117	78	0·01
Lack of energy	119	83	0·01
Self-depreciation	87	57	0·01
Depression of mood—feeling sad or low	142	108	0·01
Weeping in last month	100	63	0·01
Unvarying depression	52	28	0·01
Depression with a distinct quality	52	28	0·01
Irritable with other people	120	83	0·01
Obsessional symptoms—overall rating	55	30	0·01
Inability to make decisions	106	79	0·02
Difficulty getting on with others	77	52	0·02
Future seems bleak or hopeless	105	78	0·02
Obsessional rituals	14	3	0·02
Phobic anxiety in crowds	35	20	0·05
Feeling of being imposed on by others	61	42	0·05
Feeling of being overwhelmed with problems	96	67	0·05
Wanting to stay away from others	112	89	0·05
Depression worse in mornings	50	31	0·05
Insomnia	156	132	0·05
Loss of former interests	108	82	0·05
Own thoughts seem to be broadcast	16	6	0·05
BEHAVIOURAL RATINGS:			
Weeping	43	23	0·02
Asthenic body build	28	14	0·05

exception is thought broadcasting, a symptom almost pathognomonic of
schizophrenia, but this only predominates at the 5 per cent level and, in
isolation, its significance is unclear. Of the items which do predominate in
the Brooklyn patients few have strong diagnostic implications. But the

general impression conveyed is one of schizophrenic symptomatology, in spite of the paucity of florid psychotic phenomena like hallucinations and delusions. Behavioural abnormalities noted by the psychiatrist, as opposed to symptoms complained of by the patient, are relatively more common in the Brooklyn patients and the difference between the 'behavioural abnormalities' section scores [see TABLE 17] suggests that this is a genuine difference and not due to differences in rating threshold between the New York and London psychiatrists. The frequency of finger tremor in the Brooklyn patients is difficult to explain. It is unlikely to be a manifestation of anxiety because it was rarely accompanied by tachycardia or other evidence of arousal; probably it was caused by phenothiazines in some patients, and by alcohol withdrawal in others. The frequency of the unkempt appearance rating at Brooklyn is a reflection of differences in the milieu of the two hospitals, rather than in the patients themselves; anyone admitted to Brooklyn is routinely deprived of his or her clothes and dressed instead in garments supplied by the hospital. The predominance of financial worries at Brooklyn, in spite of the predominance of worrying in general at Netherne, is presumably due to the protection afforded in England by the provisions of the Welfare State.

The interpretation of differences between Brooklyn and Netherne on history items is much harder than for mental state items, because many of them reflect social and cultural differences between London and New York, and differences in the psychiatric services available in the two cities, as well as purely psychiatric differences. None the less, they are an important part of the picture. TABLE 19A lists those items which are significantly more common in the Brooklyn patients, and TABLE 19B the smaller number which predominate in the Netherne patients.

A comparison of the personal history items in these two tables makes it clear that the outcasts and failures of society and the chronically handicapped are much commoner at Brooklyn. More are unemployed, more are divorced, more are living alone, more have a history of delinquency or alcoholism, and more are in poor physical health. At Netherne, on the other hand, more are white-collar workers, more have steady jobs, and more have an obsessional or anankastic personality, with its implications of respectability and conformity. To some extent these differences reflect nothing more profound than the fact that, in the United States, State hospitals cater mainly for the economically unsuccessful whereas British mental hospitals cater for the bulk of the population. But to some extent they also reflect more general social differences between the two catchment areas and between the two countries. For instance, failure to finish college is common in the United States, for a variety of reasons, financial or educational. But in the United Kingdom, where university education is less widespread and largely financed from public funds, drop-out is less common and is often of psychiatric significance.

An equally clear contrast is depicted by the present illness items. Because the majority of admissions to New York State hospitals are from receiving

TABLE 19A

ALL 250 BROOKLYN PATIENTS *V.* ALL 250 NETHERNE PATIENTS.
HISTORY ITEMS SIGNIFICANTLY COMMONER IN THE
BROOKLYN PATIENTS

| | TOTAL NUMBER | | |
	BROOKLYN	NETHERNE	*p*
PERSONAL HISTORY:			
Often unemployed[1]	115	51	0·001
Currently unemployed[1]	130	76	0·001
Divorced, separated or widowed[1]	64	28	0·001
Premorbid personality, calm and placid[1]	65	28	0·001
Persistent truancy in childhood[1]	53	19	0·001
Failure to complete college education	27	7	0·001
History of serious adult crime[1]	44	18	0·001
History of addiction to alcohol	38	13	0·001
Living alone before admission[1]	52	29	0·01
Childhood disfigurement or deformity	21	4	0·01
Never had satisfactory emotional relation-ship with sexual partner[1]	91	63	0·01
Suffering from chronic physical illness	34	16	0·02
Habitually under medical care	46	26	0·02
Below average academically at school	72	43	0·02
Frequent changes of job	81	56	0·02
Youngest child in family	81	60	0·05
Current menopausal symptoms	22	10	0·05
Post-menopausal	38	22	0·05
FAMILY BACKGROUND:			
Unusually fond of father	30	4	0·001
Unusually fond of mother	35	6	0·001
Poor relationship between parents	70	42	0·01
Father's personality energetic and forceful	86	60	0·02
Overprotected by father	23	9	0·02
Mother very religious[1]	77	51	0·02
Father very religious	49	30	0·05
Rejected by father	36	22	0·05
Mother's personality calm and placid[1]	57	37	0·05
Disliked mother	23	10	0·05
PRESENT ILLNESS:			
Transferred from another hospital[1]	171	8	0·001
Compulsory admission[1]	117	48	0·001
Symptoms substantially unchanged for years[1]	49	10	0·001
Two or more episodes previously	146	101	0·001
Admitted because obviously 'crazy'	126	66	0·001
Psychotherapy before admission[1]	22	4	0·001
Admitted for treatment of drug or alcohol addiction	56	23	0·01
Admitted because of inability to work	152	112	0·01

TABLE 19A (*cont.*)

| | TOTAL NUMBER | | |
	BROOKLYN	NETHERNE	*p*
PRESENT ILLNESS (*cont.*):			
Withdrawal from normal emotional			
contacts	151	121	0·01
Sleeping more than normal	85	54	0·01
Admitted after outbreak of violence	48	25	0·01
Received phenothiazines in the past	92	65	0·02

[1] A difference, significant at the 5 per cent level or beyond, was also found on this item in a comparison between 52 Brooklyn patients and 140 Netherne patients rated by London raters.

TABLE 19B

ALL 250 BROOKLYN PATIENTS *V.* ALL 250 NETHERNE PATIENTS. HISTORY ITEMS SIGNIFICANTLY COMMONER IN THE NETHERNE PATIENTS

| | TOTAL NUMBER | | |
	NETHERNE	BROOKLYN	*p*
PERSONAL HISTORY:			
Social Class I or II	53	19	0·001
Living with spouse[1]	131	77	0·001
Living harmoniously with spouse[1]	70	23	0·001
Left school before 17[1]	198	134	0·001
Premorbid personality, obsessional[1]	94	21	0·001
Only child[1]	31	12	0·01
Psychiatric disturbance in children	49	26	0·01
History of psychosomatic illness	44	25	0·02
FAMILY BACKGROUND:			
No father, or father substitute not a			
blood relative	39	23	0·05
No mother, or mother substitute not a			
blood relative	25	12	0·05
PRESENT ILLNESS:			
Treatment by general practitioner before			
admission[1]	137	79	0·001
Antidepressive drugs before admission[1]	73	23	0·001
Previous episodes treated with anti-			
depressive drugs[1]	56	17	0·001
Major psychological stress in last year	67	34	0·001
Previous episodes with full recovery	75	48	0·01
ECT before admission[1]	39	20	0·05

NOTE: The significance levels quoted are derived from chi-square tests. In some cases here the totals refer to ratings of 1 and 2 combined.

[1] A difference, significant at the 5 per cent level or beyond, was also found on this item in a comparison between 52 Brooklyn patients and 140 Netherne patients rated by London raters.

hospitals, rather than directly from the community, and are legally enforced, many more Brooklyn patients are recorded as 'transferred from another hospital' and 'compulsory admission'. Moreover, because in London most people are registered with general practitioners, and extensive psychiatric out-patient services are available, twice as many Netherne patients are recorded as 'treated by general practitioner before admission', 'given anti-depressive drugs before admission', and 'given ECT before admission'. During the course of the study the project staff formed the impression that there were more crisis admissions at Brooklyn and also more admissions of patients with chronic disabilities, either personality disorders or schizophrenic defect states. The impression is confirmed by the preponderance in Brooklyn patients of the three items: 'symptoms substantially unchanged for years', 'admitted after outbreak of violence', and 'admitted because obviously "crazy" '. By contrast, Netherne patients show a preponderance of: 'previous episodes with full recovery', 'previous episodes treated with antidepressive drugs', and 'major stress in last year', suggesting that more of them have recurrent episodes of depression which respond to treatment.

Interpretation is hardest of all for the family background items, many of which appear to predominate in the New York patients. Because of the difficulty of defining criteria for the complex judgements involved in items such as these a comparison, analogous to that described on pages 63–4 for the mental state section scores, was carried out between the 52 Brooklyn patients and 140 Netherne patients whose history ratings had been made by one of the three London-based psychiatrists. Items for which a significant difference emerged in this comparison are marked with a superior figure 1 in TABLES 19A and B, and few of the family background items are so marked. Partly for this reason, and partly because many of the items concerned are difficult to reconcile with one another, or with the more tangible personal history items, it should probably be assumed that most of these family background differences are spurious, i.e. that they are produced by a difference in rating threshold between the London and New York teams.

Both patients and their mothers are recorded as being of calm and placid disposition more frequently in the Brooklyn series than in the Netherne series. In both cases the same preponderance was found when the comparison was restricted to patients rated by members of the London team, so it seems unlikely that rater differences are responsible. Yet it is difficult to believe that these differences are genuine. The citizens of New York are not notably less excitable than their London counterparts, and the profile established by the other items predominating in the Brooklyn series is hardly compatible with a reputation for equanimity. The ratings in question, it will be recalled, were based on the free comments of the patient and the informant in response to non-directive probes of the 'What was he like to live with?' type. Perhaps the most likely explanation is that the words 'calm' and 'placid' are used in rather different senses by Londoners and New Yorkers, implying marked equanimity to the former, but no more than the absence of any conspicuous tendency to flare up to the latter. This explanation is conjectural, but it is worth bearing in mind that there may be other spurious differences elsewhere in this study produced by subtle language differences of this sort. Words which clearly have different meanings in the common parlance of the two countries, like 'mad' and 'sick', cause little trouble. The difference in usage is known, or soon becomes apparent. Only if the difference is more subtle does it escape detection and survive to distort the results in the way that has probably occurred here.

After the completion of these comparisons between the entire Brooklyn and Netherne patient populations analogous comparisons were carried out between Brooklyn and Netherne patients with a project diagnosis of schizophrenia, and between Brooklyn and Netherne patients with a project diagnosis of affective illness. This was done partly to detect differences in symptoms within these broad diagnostic categories—to see, for instance, whether guilt feelings and self-blame were equally common in American and British depressives, or whether thought disorder was equally common in American and British schizophrenics—and partly as a further check on the consistency of the project diagnoses.

Eighty-one (32 per cent) of the Brooklyn patients and 65 (26 per cent) of the Netherne patients had a final project diagnosis of schizophrenia (categories 295·0 to 295·9 in ICD 8). TABLE 20 lists the section scores which are significantly higher and the PSE items which are significantly commoner in one or the other. There are far fewer than in the previous comparison between all the patients in each series because the populations being compared are more homogeneous and both have fewer members. Several of the items, both those predominating in Brooklyn schizophrenics and those predominating in Netherne schizophrenics, are commoner concomitants of depressive illnesses than of schizophrenia. Indeed, the only typical schizophrenic symptoms to emerge are auditory hallucinations and thought broadcasting, both of which are commoner at Netherne. This perhaps suggests that a higher proportion of the Netherne patients are overtly psychotic, but there is no predominance of other similar symptoms, like delusions of persecution and reference, or passivity feelings, and really the paucity of items predominating in either group suggests that the symptoms of the two, and the proportions of the different forms of schizophrenia in the two, are both very similar.

The corresponding comparison for history items is shown in TABLE 21. Most of the items which figure here also figure in TABLES 19A and B and 23. They are characteristic of the Brooklyn or Netherne populations as a whole, rather than of either hospital's schizophrenics, and need not be discussed any further. The predominance of the three items 'symptom free before onset of present episode', 'no previous episodes of psychiatric disturbance', and 'working full-time before admission' in Netherne schizophrenics, and of 'two or more similar episodes previously' and 'symptoms substantially unchanged

TABLE 20

81 BROOKLYN SCHIZOPHRENICS *V.* 65 NETHERNE SCHIZOPHRENICS. PSE SECTION SCORES AND ITEMS

I. SECTION SCORES AND PSE ITEMS PREDOMINATING IN BROOKLYN SCHIZOPHRENICS

	BROOKLYN	NETHERNE	p
SECTION SCORES:			
Ambiguous replies	9·84	4·31	0·05
Somatic accompaniments of depression	1·83	1·14	0·05
PSE ITEMS:			
Early morning wakening	14	2	0·02
Loss of insight	42	24	0·05
Muscular tension	24	9	0·05
Weight loss in last 3 months	33	14	0·05

2. SECTION SCORES AND PSE ITEMS PREDOMINATING IN NETHERNE SCHIZOPHRENICS

	NETHERNE	BROOKLYN	p
SECTION SCORES:			
Subjective thought disorder	1·60	0·68	0·01
Subjective memory impairment	0·98	0·51	0·05
PSE ITEMS:			
Hears voices which seem real	22	11	0·01
Own thoughts seem to be broadcast	15	5	0·01
Guilt feelings	10	2	0·02
Feeling that life is not worth living	22	13	0·05
Suicidal thoughts or attempt	20	12	0·05
Obsessional rituals	5	0	0·05
Delusional explanation of illness	20	12	0·05
Agitated and fidgeting during interview	14	7	0·05
Tachycardia during interview	23	13	0·05

for years' in the Brooklyn schizophrenics strongly suggests that the Brooklyn patients are suffering from more chronic illnesses with a greater residual defect between episodes. But although this is almost certainly a genuine difference its importance must be assessed in the light of the comparatively trivial differences found in the mental state comparison.

Ninety-one (36 per cent) of the Brooklyn patients and 118 (47 per cent) of the Netherne patients were given a final project diagnosis of some form of affective illness. Under this somewhat arbitrary rubric were included all patients with a project diagnosis of 'affective psychosis' (categories 296·0 to 296·9 in ICD 8), 'reactive depressive psychosis' (category 298·0 in ICD 8),

TABLE 21

81 BROOKLYN SCHIZOPHRENICS *V.* 65 NETHERNE SCHIZOPHRENICS.
HISTORY ITEMS

1. ITEMS SIGNIFICANTLY COMMONER IN THE BROOKLYN PATIENTS

| | TOTAL NUMBER | | |
	BROOKLYN	NETHERNE	p
PERSONAL HISTORY:			
Often unemployed	42	18	0·01
Member of non-European ethnic group	14	2	0·02
Brought up in poverty	10	1	0·02
Previous personality, always highly strung	30	12	0·05
FAMILY BACKGROUND:			
Unusually fond of father	41	12	0·001
Unusually fond of mother	46	18	0·01
Parents separated or divorced	19	4	0·01
PRESENT ILLNESS:			
Transferred from another hospital	66	3	0·001
Admitted because of inability to work	57	21	0·001
Two or more similar episodes previously	47	14	0·001
Admitted because obviously 'crazy'	65	38	0·01
Severe insomnia	40	16	0·01
Symptoms substantially unchanged for years	15	4	0·05
Sleeping more than normal	30	13	0·05

2. ITEMS SIGNIFICANTLY COMMONER IN THE NETHERNE PATIENTS

| | TOTAL NUMBER | | |
	NETHERNE	BROOKLYN	p
PERSONAL HISTORY:			
Left school before 17	49	38	0·001
Premorbid personality, obsessional	19	8	0·01
Working full-time before admission	19	10	0·02
Wealthy parents	11	3	0·05
PRESENT ILLNESS:			
Symptom free before onset of present episode	30	13	0·001
ECT before admission	16	3	0·001
No previous episodes of psychiatric disturbance	30	8	0·001
Treatment by general practitioner before admission	31	22	0·02

or 'depressive neurosis' (category 300·4 in ICD 8). The latter were included mainly because of the practical difficulty of distinguishing them from depressive psychoses. TABLE 22A lists the section scores that are significantly higher and the PSE items that are significantly commoner in the 91 Brooklyn patients. The most remarkable feature of this list is the absence of typical

TABLE 22A

91 BROOKLYN AFFECTIVES *V.* 118 NETHERNE AFFECTIVES. PSE SECTION SCORES AND ITEMS PREDOMINATING IN THE BROOKLYN PATIENTS

	BROOKLYN	NETHERNE	p
SECTION SCORES:			
Ambiguous replies	6·88	2·00	0·001
Signs of anxiety	2·64	1·64	0·001
Delusions of grandeur	0·20	0·02	0·01
Behavioural abnormalities	0·19	0·02	0·01
Blunting of affect	0·58	0·16	0·05
Incomprehensibility of speech	0·58	0·24	0·05
PSE ITEMS:			
Feels self-conscious in public	31	19	0·01
Feeling of being criticized by others	17	7	0·01
Weight gain in last 3 months	24	12	0·01
Under 30 years of age	29	18	0·02
Feeling of being accused by others	7	1	0·05
Things look grey or colourless	5	0	0·05
BEHAVIOURAL RATINGS:			
Finger tremor	42	20	0·001
Anxious facial expression	22	10	0·01
Signs of anxiety—overall rating	14	3	0·02
Complete apathy	12	4	0·02
Dysplastic body build	6	0	0·02
Blunting of affect—overall rating	8	1	0·02
Unkempt appearance	6	0	0·02
Paucity of speech	6	0	0·02
Hears accusatory voices	5	0	0·05
Believes he has special powers	7	1	0·05
Expressionless face	9	2	0·05
Very rapid speech	10	3	0·05

depressive items, but this is partly due to the higher proportion of Brooklyn patients with manic illnesses. The inclusion of manic patients inevitably lowers the average score on depressive items, and 19 per cent of the Brooklyn patients, but only 7 per cent of the Netherne patients, were predominantly manic. By the same token one would expect manic items to predominate at Brooklyn and, in fact, the 'delusions of grandeur' section score is significantly higher and the 'believes he has special powers' and 'very rapid speech' items are both significantly commoner. The preponderance of patients under the age of 30 is also due to the manic patients, who tend to be younger than depressives. Items denoting behavioural evidence of anxiety predominate at

TABLE 22B

91 BROOKLYN AFFECTIVES *V*. 118 NETHERNE AFFECTIVES. PSE SECTION SCORES AND ITEMS PREDOMINATING IN THE NETHERNE PATIENTS

	NETHERNE	BROOKLYN	*p*
SECTION SCORES:			
Depression of mood	8·21	6·53	0·01
Retardation	2·77	1·99	0·01
Loss of interests	2·19	1·60	0·05
Slowed thinking	5·22	4·04	0·05
Loss of self-esteem	3·75	2·98	0·05
Loss of concentration	2·33	1·82	0·05
PSE ITEMS:			
Loss of appetite	75	33	0·001
On sleeping tablets before admission	78	37	0·001
Neglect of personal appearance	51	18	0·001
Inability to concentrate	82	39	0·001
Lack of energy	74	34	0·01
Self-depreciation	53	25	0·01
Feeling that life is not worth living	77	39	0·01
Depression worse in mornings	38	13	0·01
Irritable with other people	59	28	0·01
Inability to relax	42	16	0·01
Severe or constant worrying	48	22	0·02
Phobic avoidance—overall rating	42	20	0·05
Inability to keep up with things	37	16	0·05
Loss of self-confidence	73	40	0·05
Depression of mood—feeling sad or low	86	48	0·05
Unvarying depression	36	15	0·05
Insomnia	87	54	0·05
Loss of ability to enjoy things	54	28	0·05
Subjective memory disturbance	66	33	0·05
BEHAVIOURAL RATINGS:			
Weeping	33	11	0·01

Brooklyn, but they are not accompanied by any of the typical symptoms of anxiety states and their significance is unclear. Several schizophrenic symptoms, like blunting of affect and incomprehensibility of speech, also appear, but it should be noted that the differences, though statistically significant, are all based on a very small number of patients. The emergence of these

TABLE 23A

91 BROOKLYN AFFECTIVES *V.* 118 NETHERNE AFFECTIVES. HISTORY
ITEMS SIGNIFICANTLY COMMONER IN THE BROOKLYN PATIENTS

	TOTAL NUMBER		
	BROOKLYN	NETHERNE	p
PERSONAL HISTORY:			
Often unemployed	30	17	0·01
Currently unemployed	35	25	0·01
Divorced, separated, or widowed	23	10	0·01
Persistent truancy in childhood	16	6	0·01
Failure to complete college education	12	3	0·01
Abuse of barbiturates or tranquillizers	24	11	0·01
Never had satisfactory emotional relation-ship with sexual partner	28	19	0·02
History of serious adult crime	10	1	0·02
Suffering from chronic physical illness	16	7	0·02
Habitually under medical care	21	12	0·02
Living alone	22	13	0·02
Frequent changes of job	24	16	0·05
Premorbid personality, calm and placid	25	16	0·05
FAMILY BACKGROUND:			
Father very religious	24	9	0·001
Unusually fond of mother	17	4	0·001
Frightened of father	26	12	0·01
Father quick tempered	21	10	0·02
Parents separated or divorced	31	22	0·02
Serious jealousies with siblings	21	12	0·02
Father prone to mood swings	23	13	0·05
Mother prone to mood swings	23	12	0·05
Mother calm and placid	22	15	0·05
Mother very religious	27	20	0·05
PRESENT ILLNESS:			
Transferred from another hospital	58	4	0·001
Compulsory admission	42	14	0·001
Admitted because obviously 'crazy'	41	23	0·001
Received phenothiazines in the past	36	25	0·01
Facetious or jovial before admission	13	4	0·01
Admitted for treatment of alcohol or drug addiction	8	1	0·02
Received psychotherapy in the past	15	8	0·05

schizophrenic items does, however, help to dispose of the possibility that the differences in project diagnoses between Brooklyn and Netherne—the higher proportion of schizophrenics at Brooklyn and of affective illnesses at Netherne —are due to the Brooklyn raters using a broader concept of schizophrenia.

Items predominating in the 118 Netherne patients are listed in TABLE 22B. Almost without exception they are typical features of depressive illnesses and several—like retardation, loss of self-esteem, and unvarying depression—are characteristic of typical manic-depressive or endogenous depression. To some extent this is an inevitable consequence of the smaller proportion of manic patients in the series, but inspection of the actual numbers involved makes it clear that this is not the whole explanation. Most of the items listed

TABLE 23B

91 BROOKLYN AFFECTIVES *V.* 118 NETHERNE AFFECTIVES. HISTORY ITEMS SIGNIFICANTLY COMMONER IN THE NETHERNE PATIENTS

| | TOTAL NUMBER | | |
	NETHERNE	BROOKLYN	p
PERSONAL HISTORY:			
Left school before 17	95	48	0·001
Premorbid personality, obsessional	51	7	0·001
Living harmoniously with spouse	43	17	0·01
Social Class I or II	26	7	0·02
Only child	16	3	0·05
FAMILY BACKGROUND:			
No mother, or mother substitute not a blood relation	16	2	0·01
No father, or father substitute not a blood relation	24	8	0·05
PRESENT ILLNESS:			
Previous episodes treated with anti-depressive drugs	39	11	0·001
Treatment by general practitioner before admission	68	34	0·01
Antidepressive drugs before admission	51	17	0·01

in TABLE 22B are present in twice as many Netherne patients as Brooklyn patients. There are, of course, more Netherne patients with depressive illnesses, but not twice as many. One must conclude, therefore, that the Netherne depressives are not only more numerous, they also tend to be more deeply depressed and to have depressions of a more typical manic-depressive or endogenous type. A further implication is that the disproportionate number of Netherne patients with a project diagnosis of depression is not attributable to the London raters using a broader concept of depressive illness.

History items predominating in the Brooklyn patients are shown in TABLE 23A. Most of them are characteristic of the Brooklyn population as a whole [see TABLE 19A] and have already been discussed. The item 'facetious or jovial before admission' is a reflection of the higher proportion of manic patients. The item 'received phenothiazines in the past' may reflect either this, or the fact that many of the Brooklyn patients regarded as having affective illnesses by the project psychiatrists were regarded as schizophrenics by the psychiatrists responsible for their treatment.

The few history items predominating in the Netherne patients are listed in TABLE 23B. The disparity in the numbers of patients with obsessional premorbid personalities is striking, particularly as previous evidence [see TABLE 19B] suggests that this is a genuine difference, and not caused by differences in rater criteria.

In summary, this lengthy item by item comparison of the two populations has tended to confirm the differences suggested by the project diagnosis comparison and has not revealed any striking differences in symptoms either within, or running across, the broad diagnostic categories of schizophrenia and affective illness. The Brooklyn schizophrenics tend to be more chronically ill, with fewer acute symptoms but more evidence of residual defects than the Netherne schizophrenics. And the Netherne depressives tend to be more deeply depressed and to have more typical manic-depressive symptoms than the Brooklyn depressives. But in comparison with the great social and cultural differences between the two populations, and the very different roles played by the two hospitals in the psychiatric services of their respective cities, these differences in symptomatology and diagnosis are surprisingly small.

CHAPTER XII

DISCUSSION OF RESULTS

THE most important conclusion to be drawn from the comparison between these two series of patients is that the difference between the two sets of hospital diagnoses is mainly due to differences in the diagnostic criteria used in the two hospitals and only partly due to genuine differences in the symptoms of the patients themselves. For every major diagnostic category the difference between the proportions of patients assigned to that category by the staff psychiatrists of the two hospitals was reduced when uniform diagnostic criteria were applied, and for the key diagnosis of schizophrenia the difference was almost eliminated.

The significance of this finding depends almost entirely on the extent to which it can be generalized. If the diagnostic criteria of the Netherne psychiatrists are indeed representative of those of British psychiatrists in general, and the diagnostic criteria of the Brooklyn psychiatrists similarly representative of American psychiatrists, then the significance is very great. It implies that the large, consistent differences between American and British national diagnostic statistics are largely spurious, and also suggests that the diagnostic criteria used in the two countries are sufficiently different from one another to impair much of the communication on clinical matters taking place between them. If, on the other hand, the diagnostic criteria used in either hospital were unrepresentative of any wider body the results of this study would be of little importance to anyone other than the handful of psychiatrists directly concerned.

The diagnostic habits of the staff of any individual psychiatric hospital are likely to be determined by the example and opinions of its senior psychiatrists, perhaps half a dozen men for a hospital of average size. In some cases even one individual, either through his authority or his powers of persuasion, may exert a dominant and idiosyncratic influence. There is thus adequate opportunity for individual hospitals to produce statistics badly distorted by personal diagnostic prejudices, and examples are known on both sides of the Atlantic. It is highly unlikely that either Brooklyn or Netherne is seriously idiosyncratic in this sense. If they were the fact would be well known to other psychiatrists in the area and their diagnostic statistics would differ considerably from the national or regional average. But the issues involved here are too important for it to be sufficient just to be fairly sure that no gross deviations are present; it is necessary to have strong evidence that the criteria used by the two hospital staffs are typical of those of their colleagues elsewhere across the whole range of diagnoses. Our initial stipulation that both hospitals' diagnostic statistics should be close to the national or State average goes part of the way to meet this requirement, but only part of the way. It is possible, for instance, that unusually generous criteria for the diagnosis of a particular condition, say manic-depressive illness, might be concealed by an abnormally low prevalence of that condition in the hospital's catchment area; similarly, two idiosyncratic diagnosticians might conceal one another if one was liberally applying the same diagnosis that the other was avoiding.

It is clear, therefore, that if the conclusions arising out of this single hospital comparison are to be generalized with any confidence the study has to be supported by other evidence derived from a wider sample of hospitals and psychiatrists. This was, indeed, foreseen from the outset and the main reason why the first comparison was not itself based on a broader sample was purely practical. It was essential to establish that it was possible to interview and diagnose two series of patients in countries 3000 miles apart, and maintain adequate consistency of method while doing so, before embarking on more elaborate enterprises. The further evidence required could have been obtained in several different ways, varying in complexity and potential effectiveness. The simplest course would have been to carry out a second single hospital comparison in different parts of the two countries, perhaps with different types of hospitals and catchment areas as well. If the results of this comparison had then been the same as those of the first, each study would have powerfully supported the other. The disadvantage of this course is that, if the results of the second comparison proved to be different from those of the original one, there would be no way of telling which of the two was more likely to be of general significance. Potentially the most effective, but also the most difficult, course would have been to examine a national sample of admissions drawn from the universe of patients entering State hospitals or area mental hospitals anywhere in the two countries. The practical difficulties, though, of such an undertaking would have been formidable, and possibly crippling, particularly in the United States where the distances involved are so great. The course finally chosen was a compromise between these two extremes. It was decided to compare samples of admissions from all the hospitals serving the great conurbations of New York City and Greater London. This, it was felt, would encompass the largest populations and the largest number of hospitals our resources could cope with, and would generate data which would not only provide a valuable transatlantic comparison in their own right, but would also establish to what extent the two original hospitals, Brooklyn and Netherne, were representative at least of their respective cities.

In fact, as is described in Part 3, this second, complementary study demonstrated that Brooklyn and Netherne hospitals were indeed representative of New York and London in most important respects. In the light of this evidence the detailed findings of the Brooklyn–Netherne comparison acquire a wider significance and merit further attention. A comparison between the 'hospital' and 'project' diagnoses of the two series of patients makes it clear that the discrepancies between the two are much greater for some diagnoses than others. For alcoholism there is broad agreement between the hospital and project diagnoses in both hospitals, in spite of the lack of any widely accepted definition of alcoholism. At the other extreme, disagreement over the diagnosis of mania is almost total. At Brooklyn all but two of the 22 patients who received project diagnoses of mania had hospital diagnoses of schizophrenia. A similar but less pronounced disagreement was apparent at Netherne. Of the 14 patients who received project diagnoses of mania, six had hospital diagnoses of schizophrenia and only three hospital diagnoses of mania. Until recently the distinction between mania and schizophrenia was of prognostic rather than of immediate therapeutic importance, for both psychoses were generally treated with phenothiazines. But with the increasingly strong evidence that has accumulated in recent years that lithium salts are an effective and specific treatment for manic illnesses (Maggs, 1963; Wharton and Fieve, 1966; Bunney, Goodwin, Davis, and Fawcett, 1968) the distinction between mania and schizophrenia has become of practical importance. The evidence available here cannot determine which concept of mania is more appropriate—the very narrow one held by the hospital psychiatrists or the much broader concept of the project psychiatrists—but in the context of forecasting response to lithium, one must be superior to the other, and it would be both important and practicable to establish which that was.

Mania provides the most obvious single discrepancy between the hospital and project diagnoses, but more striking than any individual diagnostic discrepancy is the contrast between the overall patterns of diagnostic usage of the two hospitals. At Netherne diagnoses of schizophrenia and depressive psychosis are made equally frequently, both accounting for about a third of all admissions in the age range studied, and two other non-organic diagnoses, neurotic illness and personality disorder, are each made in about 10 per cent of cases. The varied presentations of functional mental illness are thus spread over at least four broad diagnostic categories. At Brooklyn, on the other hand, two-thirds of all patients are regarded by the hospital staff as schizophrenics, only 10 per cent are regarded as having depressions of either psychotic or neurotic type, and the diagnoses of neurotic illness and personality disorder are hardly used at all. The contrast can be emphasized by grouping together all affective psychoses, all neuroses, and all personality disorders. Fifty-three per cent of all patients are placed in one of these categories by the Netherne psychiatrists, but only 11 per cent by the Brooklyn psychiatrists. For the second series of 105 patients below the age of 35 the contrast is even greater—57 per cent at Netherne compared with a mere 3 per cent at Brooklyn.

Another way of looking at these diagnostic differences is to eliminate patients with alcoholism, drug dependence, and organic psychoses, and calculate what proportion of the remaining spectrum of functional mental illness is diagnosed as schizophrenia in each hospital. The figure for Netherne is

37 per cent, but for Brooklyn it is 78 per cent; for patients under the age of 35 the contrast is even greater—35 per cent at Netherne and 84 per cent at Brooklyn. There is no significant difference between the proportions of Brooklyn and Netherne patients with project diagnoses of schizophrenia, so these gross differences between the two sets of hospital diagnoses must be largely due to differences in diagnostic usage, particularly of the key diagnosis of schizophrenia. Of the 105 Brooklyn patients under the age of 35, 81

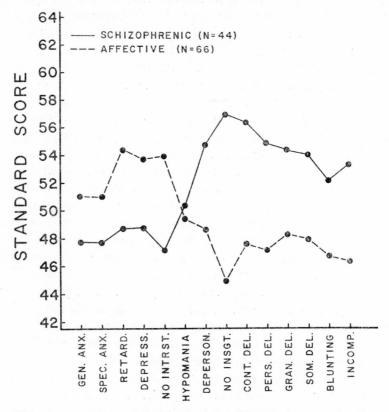

FIG. 3. The symptom profiles of the Netherne patients diagnosed by the hospital staff as schizophrenic or affective.

received a diagnosis of schizophrenia from the hospital psychiatrists and the largest number to receive any other individual diagnosis was three. In effect, a diagnosis of schizophrenia at Brooklyn is very close, at least in young adults, to being a synonym for functional mental illness and has shed most of its original symptomatic and prognostic implications. An analysis of the relationship between symptomatology and diagnosis in the first series of patients (the 145 patients in the age range 35–59) previously reported by Gurland, Fleiss, Cooper, Kendell, and Simon (1969) illustrates this. At Netherne there was a sharp contrast between the symptom profile of patients with hospital diagnoses of schizophrenia and the profile of those with hospital diagnoses of affective illness, the former having a profile high on conceptual and perceptual disorganization and low on mood disturbance, the latter a contrasting profile high on mood disturbance and low on disorganization [see FIG. 3]. At Brooklyn this contrast was not found. The schizophrenic and affective profiles were similar to one another and neither showed any marked contrast between the mood disturbance and disorganization ends of the profile [see FIG. 4].

The preceding discussion has been concerned with those differences between the hospital diagnoses of the Brooklyn and Netherne patients which were not found between the corresponding sets of project diagnoses, and so

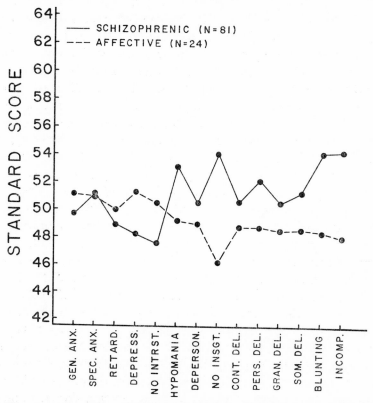

FIG. 4. The symptom profiles of the Brooklyn patients diagnosed by the hospital staff as schizophrenic or affective.

were regarded as being due simply to differences in diagnostic usage between the staffs of the two hospitals. It remains now to consider the significance of those differences which were still found when the project diagnoses were compared, and so were presumed to reflect genuine symptomatic differences between the patients themselves. Briefly, there were significantly more patients in the Netherne series with project diagnoses of manic-depressive psychosis (depressed type), depressive neurosis, anxiety neurosis, and affective illness as a whole; and significantly more patients in the Brooklyn series with project diagnoses of delirium tremens and alcoholic disorders as a whole. (All of these differences were statistically significant at the 5 per cent level, though none was great enough to be significant at the 1 per cent level [see TABLE 14].)

Although we have strong grounds for regarding these differences as genuine so far as these particular series of patients are concerned, no conclusions about the prevalence of alcoholism and depressive illness in the two communities can be drawn from them. They cannot be taken as evidence that depressions are commoner in London than in New York and alcoholism commoner in New York than in London, much less that corresponding differences exist between the United States and Great Britain. Even if such conclusions were carefully restricted to the catchment areas of the hospitals concerned they would still be unjustified. There is abundant evidence that only a small proportion of the mental illness in a community is treated in public mental hospitals, or even in hospital at all, and it is also well known that social factors may be as, or more, important than strictly medical ones in determining whether potential patients are admitted to hospital. Although there are no adequate statistics available for the private sector it is known that in New York a high proportion of people from the upper half of the social scale are treated either in private hospitals or by physicians in private office practice, instead of in public hospitals. It is also known that, at least in comparison with other types of mental illness, depressive illnesses are commoner in professional and managerial occupations than in manual workers (Clark, 1949; Jaco, 1960). It can, therefore, be confidently assumed that in New York, to a much greater extent than in London, there is a selective loss of upper-class patients to the private sector and that this involves a disproportionate loss of depressive illness. This consideration alone may well be adequate to account for the greater number of depressive illnesses in the Netherne series.

Similar considerations apply to the greater number of alcoholics in the Brooklyn series. Alcoholism, and particularly admission to hospital with alcoholism, is commoner in lower social classes, so the excess of alcoholics at Brooklyn may be simply a function of the selective loss of upper social class patients to private agencies. In any case, the admission of alcoholics to hospital is affected by social factors and selective admission policies even more strongly than mental illness as a whole, which makes any argument from admission rates to prevalence even more hazardous than usual.

PART 3. THE NEW YORK–LONDON
COMPARISON

CHAPTER XIII

THE DESIGN OF THE STUDY

THE reasons for undertaking a comparison of patients entering hospital in London and New York as a whole were outlined in the previous chapter. It was clearly necessary to carry out a second Anglo-American comparison in order to find out how representative were the striking results of the Brooklyn–Netherne comparison. For the reasons already discussed a study based on random sampling from large defined populations was felt to be preferable to a further single hospital comparison, or even to a series of such comparisons. The ideal population would have been the universe of hospitals contributing to the national diagnostic statistics of the two countries, but it seemed that the practical difficulties of such an undertaking would be likely to prove insuperable. A comparison between the two great conurbations of New York City and Greater London was therefore undertaken, on the grounds that these were the greatest population units and included the largest number of hospitals our resources were capable of coping with. The two areas had the further advantages of being geographically compact and readily accessible to the existing offices of the project staff, and also of being clearly defined administrative units of similar size and population and occupying similar roles in the economy and national life of the two countries.

New York City and Greater London both contain about eight million people. In New York this population is served by nine public mental hospitals —eight large State hospitals and the Psychiatric Institute of the State Department of Mental Hygiene. In London mental hospitals are smaller and more numerous; altogether 22 area hospitals are involved, though the catchment areas of several of these extend well beyond the boundaries of Greater London. In each city the sample was restricted to these hospitals, because they are the only ones to contribute to the diagnostic statistics compiled by the State Department of Mental Hygiene in Albany and the Ministry of Health in London. In any case, it would hardly have been feasible, given the project's limited resources, to include private hospitals or the numerous psychiatric units in general hospitals.

On statistical grounds it was decided that a sample of between 150 and 200 patients from each city would be adequate. The sampling procedures used in both cities were designed with the intention of allowing every patient admitted to any of the relevant hospitals an equal chance of being picked; but because of the differences in the size and number of the hospitals in London and New York rather different procedures were used in each.

In New York all nine hospitals contributed to the sample, and the number of patients seen at each was proportional to that hospital's admission rate in the 20–59 age range for the previous year. This meant that the contributions of individual hospitals to the sample varied greatly, from the Central Islip State Hospital with 40 patients to the Psychiatric Institute with just three.

TABLE 24

THE NINE HOSPITALS CONTRIBUTING TO THE NEW YORK SAMPLE

	TOTAL ADMISSIONS AGED 20–59 IN 1966	NUMBER OF PATIENTS FROM EACH HOSPITAL
Bronx State Hospital	1302	19
Brooklyn State Hospital	1213	14
Central Islip State Hospital	3882	40
Creedmoor State Hospital	2801	31
King's Park State Hospital	1602	17
Manhattan State Hospital	1343	20
Pilgrim State Hospital	3214	29
Psychiatric Institute	255	3
Rockland State Hospital	1477	19
	TOTAL:	*192*

The required number of patients for each hospital were picked randomly from all admissions in the appropriate age range over a 7-day period; in practice this generally involved seeing about half of that week's admissions. The nine hospitals and their respective contributions are shown in TABLE 24; the total number of patients in the sample was 192.

In London it was both impracticable and unnecessary to draw patients from all 22 hospitals. Four hospitals were eliminated on the grounds that less than 40 per cent of their catchment population lived within the boundary of Greater London, and nine hospitals were chosen from the remaining 18. Because mental hospital admission rates vary considerably from one part of a city to another (the admission rates for schizophrenia and alcoholism in particular being higher, both proportionately and absolutely, in the run-down central areas than in the suburbs) the sample was stratified geographically. This was done by dividing the 18 hospitals into three groups of six according to the location of their catchment areas—those responsible for the central areas in one group, those responsible for the outer suburbs in another, and those with mixed or intermediate catchment areas in the third. Three hospitals were then drawn from each of these groups, using a weighting procedure which gave the hospitals with the largest admission rates in the appropriate age range the best chance of being selected. As in New York, the number of patients seen at each hospital was kept proportional to that hospital's

TABLE 25

THE 22 AREA MENTAL HOSPITALS FROM WHICH THE LONDON
SAMPLE WAS DRAWN

	TOTAL ADMISSIONS AGED 20–59 1966	PERCENTAGE OF CATCHMENT POPULATION IN GREATER LONDON	LOCATION OF CATCHMENT AREA	NUMBER OF PATIENTS FROM EACH HOSPITAL
Bexley Hospital	1350	100	Mixed	21
Cane Hill Hospital	971	100	Mixed	0
Friern Hospital	1427	100	Central	24
Goodmayes Hospital	938	100	Mixed	15
Horton Hospital	1175	100	Central	0
Long Grove Hospital	1037	100	Central	18
Saint Clement's Hospital	889	100	Central	0
Shenley Hospital	1112	100	Mixed	18
Springfield Hospital	1251	100	Mixed	0
Tooting Bec Hospital	875	100	Central	0
Warlingham Park Hospital	715	100	Peripheral	0
West Park Hospital	1175	100	Central	18
Banstead Hospital	1010	90	Mixed	0
Claybury Hospital	1025	82	Peripheral	18
Warley Hospital	1030	72	Peripheral	18
Napsbury Hospital	872	62	Peripheral	0
Saint Bernard's Hospital	1516	46	Peripheral	24
Netherne Hospital	1017	45	Peripheral	0
Runwell Hospital	764	25	Eliminated	—
Oakwood Hospital	712	24	Eliminated	—
Stone House Hospital	300	14	Eliminated	—
Brookwood Hospital	950	10	Eliminated	—
			TOTAL:	*174*

total admissions in the 20 to 59 age range during the previous year, but, because the hospitals themselves varied less in size, the variation was less, from a minimum of 15 to a maximum of 24. A further difference was that, because admission rates were all lower than in New York, it was feasible for consecutive admissions to be seen, without resorting to a sampling procedure. The total number of patients in the sample was 174; the hospitals and their contributions to this sample are shown in TABLE 25.

The interviewing procedures used in the New York–London comparison were basically the same as those used previously in the Brooklyn–Netherne comparison, except that the interview with a relative was eliminated and the patient's history interview shortened considerably. This was done partly for practical reasons. Our experience in the earlier study had made it clear that, even at hospitals situated within or close to their catchment areas, it was only possible to interview a minority of relatives at the hospital. Over half had either to be visited at home or could only be contacted by phone. To contact a relative for each of nearly 200 patients scattered across a large city would have been a formidable undertaking, particularly as several of the hospitals were widely separated from their catchment areas, and successive hospitals might be situated 40 miles apart on opposite sides of the city. Practical difficulties of this sort would not have been insuperable if there had been a compelling need for an interview with a relative; but an analysis of the results of the Brooklyn–Netherne comparison showed that the history made surprisingly little contribution to the final diagnosis (Simon, Gurland, Fleiss, and Sharpe, 1971). The provisional diagnosis made at the end of the mental state interview was the same as the final diagnosis in 80 per cent of cases, and the small number of changes produced by historical data between the two major categories of schizophrenia and affective illness tended to cancel one another out. (The most conspicuous group of patients whose diagnosis was changed materially by information from a relative were alcoholics who had concealed, or glossed over, their drinking.) It was, however, agreed that if the diagnosis was in serious doubt at the end of the patient interviews an interview could still be sought with a relative or friend, and this was actually done in five cases in London and two in New York.

The patient history was shortened considerably by eliminating all family history items, personality ratings, and other items with little direct relevance to diagnosis, and by concentrating solely on the patient's psychiatric history and the development of the present illness. In one respect the interview was expanded, by the addition of a special section for patients with a history of drug or alcohol abuse, but the total number of items was still greatly reduced, from 232 to 116.

Partly to compensate for the loss of general background data about the patient entailed by this pruning of the history interview, a new sociocultural history interview was introduced. This was designed to elicit from the patient basic demographic data about himself and his family—their ethnic background, religion, education, social class, income level, and so on. The interview was held after the psychiatric interviews were completed and had no bearing on the diagnosis. It was administered by a social scientist in New York and a psychiatric social worker in London, and took about 15 minutes to complete.

The mental state interview was altered in a number of minor ways for this study. The Eighth Edition of the Present State Examination was used instead of the Seventh, but the differences between the two were all fairly trivial. A few items were reworded, some new ones added, and several others eliminated because they were either rare or unreliable; as a result the total number of items was reduced from 480 to 442. At the same time 55 Psychiatric Status Schedule items that had been omitted in the original version of the combined schedule were now included in order to make Diagno diagnoses more meaningful. (Originally PSS items relevant to diagnoses of alcoholism, drug addiction, and personality disorder had been omitted and Diagno had therefore been incapable of generating diagnoses in these areas.)

TABLE 26

PATIENTS LOST TO THE LONDON SAMPLE

SEX	AGE	HOSPITAL	HOSPITAL DIAGNOSIS
Female	38	Friern	Anxiety State
Female	25	Friern	Depression
Male	39	West Park	(none given)
Male	21	Long Grove	Psychopathy
Female	35	Long Grove	Acute confusional state
Female	28	Bexley	Depression
Female	44	Warley	Schizophrenia

(All seven were lost through leaving hospital within 48 hours of admission, before being interviewed.)

PATIENTS LOST TO THE NEW YORK SAMPLE

SEX	AGE	HOSPITAL	HOSPITAL DIAGNOSIS
Male	44	Central Islip	Delirium tremens
Female	27	Bronx	Schizophrenia (undifferentiated)
Female	32	Psychiatric Institute	Psychoneurosis (anxiety state)

(The 44-year-old man was admitted in coma and died without regaining consciousness; the two women absconded before being interviewed.)

In both cities the nine hospitals were visited one after the other over the course of a few months in 1968. In London interviewing started in April and ended in August; in New York the first hospital was visited in May and the last in October. As in the previous study, there was an interchange of raters between the two cities, 20 of the New York patients being rated by one of the London-based psychiatrists and 12 of the London patients being rated by one of the New York psychiatrists. Apart from the alterations in the interview schedule described above, exactly the same interviewing and diagnostic procedures were used as in the Brooklyn–Netherne comparison. The majority of patients were seen within 24 hours and nearly all within 72 hours of admission. In New York, however, because a high proportion of State hospital admissions are initially admitted to a receiving hospital and only transferred to the State hospital a week or so later, nearly half the sample had been in hospital for over 5 days altogether before being interviewed. Sometimes the mental state and shortened history interviews were conducted in a single sitting; sometimes the history and part of the mental state were left over to the next day. A provisional diagnosis was made by the psychiatrist concerned as soon as the interviews were completed, without reference to the hospital notes, and the final diagnosis decided by a group of three psychiatrists, including the one who had interviewed the patient and usually a representative of the team on the other side of the Atlantic. The same nomenclature (ICD 8) and glossary (General Register Office, 1968) were used as before, and the same provision was made for main, subsidiary, and alternative diagnoses.

A few patients were again lost through discharging themselves, or absconding, before the project staff had a chance to interview them, and one New York patient was admitted in coma and died without regaining consciousness. The seven London patients lost in this way were replaced by others from the same hospital by taking the next admission in the 20–59 age range, but the three New York patients were not replaced. Details of these 10 are given in TABLE 26.

CHAPTER XIV

THE DEMOGRAPHIC CHARACTERISTICS
OF THE PATIENTS

THE salient demographic characteristics of the two groups of patients, as established in the sociocultural history interview, are set out in TABLE 27. There are significantly more young patients, and male patients, in the New York sample. This was not found in the Brooklyn–Netherne comparison, probably because younger and older patients were interviewed in separate series, each containing a set number of patients. Racially there are several significant differences between the two groups, though none of them is overwhelming. Twenty-nine per cent of the New York patients were Negroes, but so were 11 per cent of the London patients (mostly West Indian immigrants) and a further 6 per cent were of Indian or Mediterranean origin (mainly Pakistani and Cypriot immigrants).

The figures for immigrants reveal some interesting differences. Historically, it is New York that has always been the great 'melting pot', attracting immigrants from all over the world, while London has attracted workers from other parts of the British Isles but generally not from further afield. But in the last two decades these roles have largely been reversed and the change is reflected by these two samples of patients. A higher proportion of the London sample were born abroad and more than twice as many had immigrated after the age of 16. But those unable to speak English fluently are still commoner in the New York sample, probably because London's immigrants are mainly from Eire and the Commonwealth, whereas New York's are mostly Spanish-speaking from Puerto Rico and Latin America.

The social class differences between the two samples are surprisingly small, Hollingshead's Two Factor Index, based partly on occupation and partly on education (Hollingshead, 1965), reveals no significant difference between the two, and the only significant difference between them in terms of 'highest occupational level' is a slight excess of London patients from clerical, sales, and technical occupations. Presumably, the loss in New York of potential patients from the upper social classes to private hospitals and psychiatrists in private office practice is offset by a higher proportion of the New York population belonging to the professional and managerial classes, compared with London.

There are, however, some striking educational differences between the two samples. A far higher proportion of the London patients (67 per cent *v.* 22 per cent) had finished their formal education before the age of 16, but in spite of this and the greater number of recent immigrants in London, there

TABLE 27

THE DEMOGRAPHIC CHARACTERISTICS OF THE NEW YORK AND
LONDON PATIENTS

	NEW YORK ($N = 192$)	%	LONDON ($N = 174$)	%	p
AGE					
20s	61	32	37	21	0·05
30s	55	29	58	33	n.s.
40s	37	19	40	23	n.s.
50s	36	19	39	22	n.s.
SEX					
Male	102	53	68	39	0·01
RACE					
Caucasian—European	133	69	144	83	0·001
Caucasian—Indian or Mediterranean	0	—	10	6	0·01
Mongolian	1	1	0	—	n.s.
Negro	55	29	20	11	0·001
IMMIGRANT STATUS					
Born outside USA/UK	32	17	51	29	0·01
Immigrated after age 16	23	12	47	27	0·001
Lived in New York/ London under 10 yrs.	38	20	42	24	n.s.
Native language English	160	83	157	90	n.s.
Poor command of English	23	12	8	5	0·05
SOCIAL CLASS (Hollingshead Two Factor Index)					
I	1	1	1	1	⎫
II	5	3	5	3	⎪
III	27	14	11	6	⎬ n.s.
IV	69	36	76	44	⎪
V	83	43	68	39	⎪
Unclassifiable	7	4	13	7	⎭
HIGHEST OCCUPATIONAL LEVEL					
Professional or executive	7	4	7	4	n.s.
Minor professional, etc.	21	11	11	6	n.s.
Clerical, technical, etc.	43	22	56	32	0·05
Skilled manual	29	15	21	12	n.s.
Semiskilled manual	53	28	46	26	n.s.
Unskilled manual	29	15	26	15	n.s.
Unclassifiable	10	5	7	4	

TABLE 27 (*cont.*)

	NEW YORK (N = 192)	%	LONDON (N = 174)	%	p
EDUCATION					
Less than 8 years' schooling	35	18	12	7	0·01
Education ceased before 16	43	22	116	67	0·001
University (college) education	7	4	3	2	n.s.
MARITAL STATUS					
Single	72	38	50	29	n.s.
Married	59	31	96	55	0·001
Widowed	10	5	7	4	n.s.
Divorced or Separated	51	27	21	12	0·001
Married more than once	35	18	7	4	0·001
RELIGIOUS BACKGROUND					
Protestant	78	41	105	60	0·001
Catholic	86	45	40	23	0·001
Jewish	15	8	2	1	0·01
Other	13	7	27	16	

are more than twice as many patients in the New York series with less than 8 years' schooling. Presumably, this is a reflection of the greater ease with which children escape from, or drop out of, the school system in New York. The proportion with a college education is small in both cities, but the New York figure must be affected considerably by the loss of upper social class patients to private hospitals.

As in the Brooklyn–Netherne study a much higher proportion of the London patients are married, and a correspondingly higher proportion of the New York patients divorced or separated, or unmarried. More of the New York patients have been married more than once as well. Finally, there are significantly more Catholics and Jews in the New York sample and more Protestants in the London sample, but the differences are not as gross as in the earlier Brooklyn–Netherne comparison where the individual character-istics of the two hospitals' catchment areas were playing an important part. The same can probably be said of all the social and cultural differences between these two series—they are generally less marked than the correspond-ing differences in the Brooklyn–Netherne study, because New York and London taken as a whole are less dissimilar than the catchment areas of the two original hospitals.

CHAPTER XV

THE CONSISTENCY OF THE PROJECT DIAGNOSIS

As in the Brooklyn–Netherne study, checks were made on the all-important issue of the consistency of the project diagnosis. This time it was not worth examining the diagnoses made by the project psychiatrists when they crossed over between London and New York, because the number of patients involved—12 in London and 20 in New York—was not large enough. But the two other procedures used previously—the logical decision tree program, Diagno I, and the rediagnosis on the basis of canonical variate scores—were not dependent on rater cross-over and were both used again.

Diagno diagnoses were generated for all 366 patients. Because of the 55 additional PSS items (covering alcoholism, drug addiction, and antisocial behaviour) that had been added to the mental state interview, it was possible this time for Diagno to generate a full range of diagnoses. These were still not fully comparable with the project diagnosis, because they were derived from a different nomenclature (DSM I) and because the concepts of schizophrenia and affective illness embodied in Diagno differed considerably in scope from those of the project diagnosis. However, as was explained before [p. 49], these differences were not really important for our purposes. The project and Diagno diagnoses were not required to be the same; all that mattered was that the New York/London ratio should be similar for the two. The two sets of diagnoses and the ratios derived from them are shown in TABLE 28. For schizophrenia the Diagno New York/London ratio is higher than the project ratio, whereas for affective illness and alcoholism it is the project New York/London ratio which is the higher of the two. This suggests that the project psychiatrists in New York may have been using a narrower concept of schizophrenia, but rather broader concepts of affective illness and alcoholism, than their colleagues in London.

Similar implications emerged from the canonical variate analysis. A slightly different set of items had to be used for the analysis this time because of the elimination of several of the history items used previously. In fact, 47 items were used in all, of which 35 were the same as before. Forty were PSE items and the remainder from the history; again, they were chosen for their relevance to the distinctions between the three diagnostic groupings of schizophrenia, affective psychosis and neurosis. Full details of the analysis will not be given because the principles involved and the techniques employed were the same as before. Two canonical variates were obtained and the effect of rediagnosing the 265 patients with project diagnoses of schizophrenia, affective psychosis or neurosis on the basis of their scores on these variates is shown in TABLE 29. As before, about 20 per cent of the patients received scores on the two variates which placed them in a different diagnostic grouping from their project diagnosis, but most of these changes tended to balance one another

TABLE 28

PROJECT AND DIAGNO I DIAGNOSES FOR THE NEW YORK AND LONDON SAMPLES

| | NEW YORK | | LONDON | |
	DIAGNO	PROJECT	DIAGNO	PROJECT
Schizophrenia (including paranoid states)	86	56	78	61
Affective illness (including depressive neuroses)	26	62	48	76
Alcoholism	35	44	8	8
Other diagnoses	45	30	40	29

SCHIZOPHRENIA

    Diagno New York/London ratio = 1·10
    Project New York/London ratio = 0·92

AFFECTIVE ILLNESS

    Diagno New York/London ratio = 0·54
    Project New York/London ratio = 0·82

ALCOHOLISM

    Diagno New York/London ratio = 4·38
    Project New York/London ratio = 5·50

TABLE 29

THE APPLICATION OF CRITERIA DERIVED FROM CANONICAL VARIATE SCORES TO THE PROJECT DIAGNOSES OF NEW YORK AND LONDON PATIENTS

	A	B	C	D
New York schizophrenics	56	−5	+6	57
New York psychotic affectives	49	−19	+11	41
New York neurotics	16	−6	+13	23
TOTAL:	*121*	*−30*	*+30*	*121*
London schizophrenics	61	−8	+3	56
London psychotic affectives	51	−12	+12	51
London neurotics	32	−5	+10	37
TOTAL:	*144*	*−25*	*+25*	*144*

A = Project diagnosis
B = Patients with scores on the two variates outside the appropriate range
C = Additional patients with scores on the variates within the appropriate range
D = Final total ('canonical variate diagnosis')

out. The overall effect on the New York sample was to increase the number of schizophrenics by 1 to 57, to increase the number of neurotics by 7 to 23, and to reduce the psychotic affectives by 8 to 41. For the London patients the pattern of changes was rather different; the number of neurotics was increased by 5 to 37, the number of schizophrenics was reduced by 5 to 56, and the number of psychotic affectives remained unchanged. The increase in the size of the neurotic group is unimportant in itself, because it is much the same for both. But the fact that it takes place at the expense of schizophrenics in the London series but of psychotic affectives in the New York series suggests that the project criteria for a diagnosis of schizophrenia were rather broader in London than in New York, and the other way about for a diagnosis of affective psychosis.

TABLE 30

THE EFFECT ON THE PROJECT DIAGNOSES OF APPLYING THE
CRITERIA DERIVED FROM CANONICAL VARIATE SCORES

	BROOKLYN–NETHERNE COMPARISON		NEW YORK–LONDON COMPARISON	
American schizophrenics	81	−2	56	+1
American psychotic affectives	67	+1	49	−8
American neurotics	35	+1	16	+7
English schizophrenics	65	−4	61	−5
English psychotic affectives	79	−7	51	+0
English neurotics	60	+11	32	+5

Thus, both Diagno and this canonical variate analysis carry essentially the same implications for the consistency of the project diagnosis. As the two depend upon quite different mathematical principles, and in this instance also were based on completely different sets of items, the transatlantic differences they reveal are likely to be genuine. It is important to appreciate though, that these differences are small in comparison with the differences between project diagnoses and hospital diagnoses; without the use of these specialized techniques they could probably never have been detected at all. They could not, for instance, have been inferred from the detailed comparison of the symptoms of the two samples described in CHAPTER XVII. Moreover, the apparent differences between the criteria used for the project diagnoses in London and New York are not the same as those revealed by canonical variate analysis in the Brooklyn–Netherne study. As TABLE 30 shows, the pattern of changes produced by rediagnosing patients on the basis of their canonical variate scores is quite different in the two studies; in the first it is the London raters who have a disproportionately broad concept of affective psychosis, but in the second it is the New York raters. The identity of the psychiatrists involved, and the formal rules for producing the project diagnosis, were substantially the same in both studies; and a conscious attempt at compensating for earlier disparities was not responsible, because the results of the canonical variate analysis of the Brooklyn–Netherne data were not available at the time the New York–London study was carried out. It would have been more serious had the same transatlantic differences been revealed in both studies. As it is, the differences that were detected are probably attributable mainly to fluctuations over time in the diagnostic criteria of individual raters, and to chance differences in the range of patient types seen by individual raters in the two studies.

CHAPTER XVI

DIFFERENCES IN DIAGNOSIS BETWEEN THE TWO SAMPLES

THE main reason why Brooklyn State Hospital and Netherne Hospital were originally chosen for the first study was that their diagnostic statistics were close to their respective regional or national averages. The rationale for this stipulation was that it suggested that there was probably nothing unusual either about the catchment areas or admission policies of these hospitals, or about the diagnostic criteria used by their psychiatrists. This was important

TABLE 31

A COMPARISON OF THE DIAGNOSTIC COMPOSITIONS OF THE BROOKLYN SERIES AND THE SAMPLE OF PATIENTS FROM ALL NINE NEW YORK HOSPITALS

| | BROOKLYN | | | NEW YORK | |
	Hospital Diagnoses %	Project Diagnoses %		Project Diagnoses %	Hospital Diagnoses %
Schizophrenia	65·2	32·4		29·2	61·5
Depressive psychoses	7·2	18·0		19·8	4·7
Mania	0·8	8·8		5·7	0·5
Depressive neuroses	2·4	9·6		6·8	1·6
Other neuroses	0·4	4·4		1·6	2·6
Personality disorders	0·8	3·2		4·2	1·0
Alcoholic disorders	12·4	11·6	**	22·9	19·8
Drug dependence	1·2	3·2		3·1	0·0
Organic psychoses	2·8	3·6		2·6	5·2
Other diagnoses	6·8	5·2		4·2	3·1
	n = 250			n = 192	

NOTE: Here, and in the following tables, ** indicates that the difference between the two percentages is statistically significant at the 1 per cent level (using critical ratios) and * that it is significant at the 5 per cent level.

because any attempt to draw general conclusions from the results of this study implicitly assumes that both hospitals are fairly representative in these respects.

The diagnostic composition of the patient samples drawn in this present study from all of London's and New York's mental hospitals can be used to test the validity of these earlier assumptions; at least, they can be used to assess how representative Brooklyn and Netherne were of their respective cities, if not of their respective countries. TABLE 31 shows the hospital and project diagnoses of the Brooklyn patients compared with those of the 192 patients in the New York sample. The only significant difference between the two sets of project diagnoses is for alcoholic disorders, where the proportion is twice as high (23 per cent *v.* 12 per cent) for the city sample; in all other respects the two sets of percentages are very similar. The same is true for the two sets of hospital diagnoses: there are more alcoholics in the New York sample but otherwise the two sets of figures are almost the same. Provided

TABLE 32

A COMPARISON OF THE DIAGNOSTIC COMPOSITIONS OF THE NETHERNE SERIES AND THE SAMPLE OF PATIENTS DRAWN FROM NINE DIFFERENT LONDON HOSPITALS

| | NETHERNE | | | LONDON | |
	Hospital Diagnoses %	*Project Diagnoses* %		*Project Diagnoses* %	*Hospital Diagnoses* %
Schizophrenia	34·0	26·0	*	35·1	33·9
Depressive psychoses	32·8	26·0		23·0	24·1
Mania	1·6	5·6		6·3	6·9
Depressive neuroses	4·0	15·6		14·4	8·0
Other neuroses	8·0	8·4		4·0	5·7
Personality disorders	8·4	4·8		3·4	4·6
Alcoholic disorders	4·4	6·4		4·6	3·4
Drug dependence	2·0	2·8		0·6	0·6
Organic psychoses	2·0	1·6		3·4	1·7
Other diagnoses	2·8	2·8		5·2	10·9
	$n = 250$			$n = 174$	

one assumes that project diagnoses were made to consistent criteria throughout, two conclusions follow from this. Except for a deficiency of alcoholics, Brooklyn's patients were indeed representative of New York City; and, equally, the diagnostic criteria of the Brooklyn psychiatrists were typical of those of the staffs of the rest of the city's State hospitals.

The corresponding comparison between the Netherne series and the London sample is shown in TABLE 32. In general, the two sets of project diagnoses are very similar to one another, but there is one significant difference. Only 26 per cent of the Netherne patients were diagnosed as schizophrenics, compared with 35 per cent of the London sample. Netherne's catchment area is on the periphery of Greater London and it is well established that admission rates for schizophrenia are higher, both proportionately and absolutely, in the run-down central areas of big cities than in the surrounding suburbs. It is therefore to be expected, on these grounds alone, that a series of patients from Netherne should contain a lower proportion of schizophrenics than a sample drawn from the city as a whole. But the hospital diagnoses of the two series indicate that there is exactly the same proportion of schizophrenics (34 per cent) in both. This disparity between hospital and project diagnoses suggests either that the project criteria for a diagnosis of schizophrenia changed between the two studies, or that Netherne psychiatrists are prone to diagnose schizophrenia rather more readily than other London psychiatrists. In fact, as was discussed previously in CHAPTER X, there is independent evidence that Netherne psychiatrists have a tendency to 'over-diagnose' schizophrenia relative to other London psychiatrists (Parkes, 1963; Brown, Bone, Dalison, and Wing, 1966). Thus it appears that Netherne

TABLE 33

THE HOSPITAL DIAGNOSES OF THE LONDON AND
NEW YORK SAMPLES

	NEW YORK		LONDON	
	NO.	%	NO.	%
Schizophrenia	118	61·5	59	33·9**
Depressive psychoses	9	4·7	42	24·1**
Mania	1	0·5	12	6·9**
Depressive neuroses	3	1·6	14	8·0**
Other neuroses	5	2·6	10	5·7
Personality disorders	2	1·0	8	4·6*
Alcoholic disorders	38	19·8	6	3·4**
Drug dependence	0	—	1	0·6
Organic psychoses	10	5·2	3	1·7
Other diagnoses	6	3·1	19	10·9**
TOTAL:	*192*		*174*	

Hospital's typical diagnostic statistics, which were responsible for its choice as the original British hospital to be studied, are to some extent the product of two opposing factors—a relative lack of schizophrenics masked by a rather broad concept of schizophrenia. Incidentally, TABLE 32 also shows that the hospital and project diagnoses for the London sample are very similar to one another, at least in aggregate, which indicates that the diagnostic criteria used by the project staff are close to those of the majority of other London psychiatrists.

Turning now to the more important comparison between the 192 patients of the New York sample and the 174 of the London sample, the two sets of hospital diagnoses present much the same contrast as in the earlier Brooklyn–Netherne comparison. (As before, these diagnoses were obtained from the statistical departments of the State Department of Mental Hygiene in New York and the Ministry of Health in England, rather than directly from the hospitals themselves.) The differences between these hospital diagnoses are summarized in TABLE 33. There appear to be twice as many schizophrenics and nearly six times as many alcoholics in the New York sample, and five times as many depressives, twelve times as many manics and four times as many patients with personality disorders in the London sample. For every major diagnostic category, other than the organic psychoses, there is a statistically significant difference. But, as before, the project diagnoses present a very different picture. They are set out in detail in TABLE 34. There is

TABLE 34

THE PROJECT DIAGNOSES OF THE LONDON AND NEW YORK
SAMPLES

	NEW YORK		LONDON	
	NO.	%	NO.	%
SCHIZOPHRENIA AND PARANOID STATES				
Hebephrenic type	6	3·1	3	1·7
Catatonic type	5	2·6	2	1·1
Paranoid type	34	17·7	41	23·6
Acute schizophrenic episode	1	0·5	3	1·7
Latent schizophrenia	1	0·5	1	0·6
Residual schizophrenia	4	2·1	7	4·0
Schizo-affective type	5	2·6	2	1·1
Paranoia	—	—	2	1·1
TOTAL:	56	29·2	61	35·1
AFFECTIVE ILLNESS				
Involutional melancholia	1	0·5	3	1·7
MD psychosis, depressed	33	17·2	31	17·8
Reactive depressive psychosis	1	0·5	2	1·1
Depressive neurosis	13	6·8	25	14·4*
MD psychosis, manic	11	5·7	11	6·3
Affective psychosis, unspecified	3	1·6	3	1·7
Reactive excitation	—	—	1	0·6
TOTAL:	62	32·3	76	43·7*
NEUROSES (OTHER THAN DEPRESSIVE)				
Anxiety neurosis	2	1·0	2	1·1
Hysterical neurosis	1	0·5	—	—
Phobic neurosis	—	—	1	0·6
Neurasthenia	—	—	3	1·7
Hypochondriacal neurosis	—	—	1	0·6
TOTAL:	3	1·6	7	4·0
PERSONALITY DISORDERS				
Affective type	—	—	3	1·7
Schizoid type	1	0·5	—	—
Explosive type	3	1·6	—	—
Hysterical type	1	0·5	1	0·6
Asthenic type	1	0·5	1	0·6
Antisocial type	1	0·5	—	—
Other types	1	0·5	—	—
TOTAL:	8	4·2	5	2·9

TABLE 34 (*cont.*)

	NEW YORK		LONDON	
	NO.	%	NO.	%
ALCOHOLIC DISORDERS				
Habitual excessive drinking	8	4·2	1	0·6*
Alcoholic addiction	27	14·1	6	3·4**
Delirium tremens	2	1·0	—	—
Other alcoholic hallucinoses	3	1·6	1	0·6
Alcoholic paranoia	1	0·5	—	—
Other alcoholic psychoses	3	1·6	—	—
TOTAL:	44	22·9	8	4·6**
DRUG DEPENDENCE				
Opium derivatives	3	1·6	—	—
Other drugs	3	1·6	1	0·6
TOTAL:	6	3·1	1	0·6
ORGANIC PSYCHOSES				
With cerebral syphilis	1	0·5	—	—
With epilepsy	1	0·5	—	—
With brain trauma	1	0·5	—	—
With drug intoxication	2	1·0	2	1·1
Other organic psychoses	—	—	4	2·3
TOTAL:	5	2·6	6	3·4
OTHER DIAGNOSES				
Mental retardation	1	0·5	2	1·1
Transient situational disturbance	1	0·5	3	1·7
Sexual deviation	—	—	1	0·6
Non-psychotic disorder with other physical condition	—	—	1	0·6
Acute paranoid reaction	—	—	1	0·6
Anorexia nervosa	—	—	1	0·6
Reactive psychosis, unspecified	1	0·5	1	0·6
No psychiatric abnormality	2	1·0	—	—
No diagnoses possible or made	3	1·6	—	—
TOTAL:	8	4·2	10	5·7

still a considerable excess of alcoholic disorders in the New York sample, and this is statistically significant for the category as a whole (23 per cent *v.* 5 per cent) as well as for the subcategories of habitual excessive drinking (4 per cent *v.* 1 per cent) and alcoholic addiction (14 per cent *v.* 3 per cent). There is also a moderate excess of depressive neuroses (14 per cent *v.* 7 per cent) and of affective illnesses as a whole (44 per cent *v.* 32 per cent) in the London sample, but these are the only significant differences between the two. As in the Brooklyn–Netherne study, there is no significant difference between the proportions of the two series diagnosed as schizophrenics.

Detailed examination of the two sets of diagnoses makes it clear that there is a higher proportion of London patients in most categories, largely because of the predominance of alcoholics, and to a lesser extent of drug addicts, in the New York sample. But alcoholics and drug addicts are in many ways a distinct group, set apart from the general run of functional mental illness. Their prevalence is more strongly dependent on social factors than that of mental illness as a whole, and their appearance in hospital series is more

TABLE 35

THE PROJECT DIAGNOSES OF THE LONDON AND NEW YORK
SAMPLES AFTER THE EXCLUSION OF ALCOHOLICS AND
DRUG ADDICTS

	NEW YORK		LONDON	
	NO.	%	NO.	%
Schizophrenia	56	39·4	61	37·0
Depressive psychoses	38	26·8	40	24·2
Mania	11	7·7	11	6·7
Depressive neuroses	13	9·2	25	15·2
Other neuroses	3	2·1	7	4·2
Personality disorders	8	5·6	6	3·6
Organic psychoses	5	3·5	6	3·6
Other diagnoses	8	5·6	9	5·5
TOTAL:	*142*		*165*	

dependent on administrative decisions affecting admission policies. Hence, the proportion of admissions they account for is liable to vary greatly from time to time and place to place. If, on these grounds, the alcoholics and drug addicts in both series are set aside and the remaining patients compared there are no longer any significant differences between the two samples; indeed, as TABLE 35 shows, there is a remarkable similarity between the two.

In many ways this is the most important and perhaps also the most surprising finding in this entire study. In spite of the gross differences in the diagnostic statistics produced by the hospitals of the two cities, in spite of the profound social and cultural differences between the cities themselves, and the very different roles played by State hospitals and area mental hospitals in the overall psychiatric services of these cities, in spite of all these factors, when uniform diagnostic criteria are employed the diagnostic distributions of patients entering hospital in New York and London are to all intents and purposes identical. It must not, of course, be concluded from this that the prevalence of different forms of mental illness is the same in London and New York. As has been emphasized before, conclusions about prevalence or incidence can never be drawn from a study of hospital populations alone.

Indeed, because the roles of State hospitals and area mental hospitals differ in many important respects, the fact that the diagnostic composition of their admissions is so similar could be taken to suggest quite the opposite—that there are probably important differences in the relative prevalence of different illnesses between the two cities which happen to offset the differences in the roles of the two types of hospital.

The contrast between the diagnostic criteria of New York psychiatrists and those of the project staff is clearly illustrated by the detailed breakdown of the project and hospital diagnoses of the New York sample given in TABLE 36. Overall there is exactly 50 per cent agreement between the two; but without the alcoholic disorders, for which agreement is comparatively good, this figure would be much lower. Less than half the patients with hospital diagnoses of schizophrenia have the same project diagnosis and, as the top line of the table shows, a high proportion of the patients with project diagnoses in all 10 diagnostic categories are regarded by the hospital staff as schizophrenics. Sixty-three per cent of those with a project diagnosis of depressive psychosis, 91 per cent of those with a project diagnosis of mania, 69 per cent of those with a project diagnosis of neurosis, and 63 per cent of those with a project diagnosis of personality disorder all have hospital diagnoses of schizophrenia. Indeed, it is hardly an exaggeration to say that schizophrenia is the only type of functional mental illness recognized with any frequency by the hospital psychiatrists. Excluding alcoholics and patients with organic psychoses, only 18 per cent of this sample (26 out of 144) received any other diagnosis.

The corresponding comparison for the London patients is shown in TABLE 37. Here there is no clear-cut pattern of agreement or disagreement and, in spite of the similarity in the overall distributions of the hospital and project diagnoses, only 50 per cent of patients receive the same diagnosis from both sources. Agreement between the two is best for schizophrenia and worst for depressive neurosis and personality disorders. Disagreement over depressive neurosis is an almost inevitable consequence of the Ministry of Health's coding of hospital diagnoses of 'depression' as manic-depressive depression; and disagreement over personality disorders is probably attributable to the frequency with which these co-exist with other conditions, and to the difficulty of deciding which to regard as the main diagnosis.

As a corollary to these direct comparisons between the diagnoses of the New York and London patients, the relationship between diagnosis and some of the social and demographic variables known to be associated with diagnostic trends of one sort or another was investigated separately for each sample. These studies will be reported in detail elsewhere but the salient findings were these: there was no significant relationship between social class and diagnosis in either city. This was true for both the hospital and the project diagnoses, but too much significance should not be read into this finding because the upper social classes were inadequately represented, with less than 20 per cent of either sample in any of the upper three categories of the

TABLE 36

A COMPARISON BETWEEN THE HOSPITAL AND PROJECT DIAGNOSES OF THE NEW YORK SAMPLE

HOSPITAL DIAGNOSES	MAIN PROJECT DIAGNOSES										
	Schizophrenia	Dep. Psych.	Mania	Dep. Neur.	Other Neur.	Pers. Dis.	Alcoh. Dis.	Drug Dep.	Organ. Psych.	Other Dis.	TOTAL
Schizophrenia	**50**	24	10	8	3	5	11	3	2	2	118
Depressive psychoses	1	7	—	—	—	—	—	—	—	1	9
Mania	—	1	—	—	—	—	—	—	—	—	1
Depressive neuroses	—	1	—	**2**	—	—	—	—	—	—	3
Other neuroses	1	1	—	2	—	1	1	—	—	—	5
Personality disorders	—	—	—	1	—	**1**	1	—	—	—	2
Alcoholic disorders	1	2	—	—	—	1	**32**	1	1	—	38
Drug dependence	—	—	—	—	—	—	—	—	—	—	—
Organic psychoses	2	—	1	—	—	—	—	2	**2**	3	10
Other disorders	1	3	—	—	—	—	—	—	—	2	6
TOTAL:	56	38	11	13	3	8	44	6	5	8	192

TABLE 37

A COMPARISON BETWEEN THE HOSPITAL AND PROJECT DIAGNOSES OF THE LONDON SAMPLE

HOSPITAL DIAGNOSES	MAIN PROJECT DIAGNOSES										TOTAL
	Schizo-phrenia	Dep. Psych.	Mania	Dep. Neur.	Other Neur.	Pers. Dis.	Alcoh. Dis.	Drug Dep.	Organ. Psych.	Other Dis.	
Schizophrenia	44	6	4	1	—	2	1	1	—	—	59
Depressive psychoses	6	17	2	12	1	2	—	—	2	—	42
Mania	1	5	5	—	—	—	—	—	1	—	12
Depressive neuroses	—	3	—	5	3	1	1	—	—	1	14
Other neuroses	1	5	—	1	2	—	1	—	—	—	10
Personality disorders	2	—	—	4	—	1	—	—	1	—	8
Alcoholic disorders	—	—	—	1	—	—	5	—	—	—	6
Drug dependence	1	—	—	—	—	—	—	—	—	—	1
Organic psychoses	2	1	—	—	—	—	—	—	—	—	3
Other diagnoses	4	3	—	1	1	—	—	—	2	8	19
TOTAL:	61	40	11	25	7	6	8	1	6	9	174

Hollingshead scale. There was, however, a strong relationship between diagnosis and race in both cities. In London and in New York there was a highly significant ($p < 0.005$) excess of black patients with hospital diagnoses of schizophrenia. In London this also held true for a project diagnosis of schizophrenia, but not in New York. Here, there was not even a tendency for Negroes to receive more than their share of schizophrenic diagnoses. Many different interpretations could be put on these findings, all of them speculative. We would suggest though, that the probable explanation lies along these lines. In London there is a genuine excess of schizophrenic illnesses in black patients and this is related to their cultural displacement (all 20 black patients in the London sample were first-generation immigrants, mostly from the West Indies). In New York, on the other hand, only a minority of the black population have undergone any comparable cultural transposition and there is no excess of schizophrenia, in the sense in which the term was used by the project psychiatrists. The reason why black patients attract hospital diagnoses of schizophrenia so readily in New York is unclear, though it may be due at least in part to a 'social distance' effect, and to their tendency to be suspicious, uncommunicative, and out of work. Whatever the explanation, it is a striking fact that although 23 of the 55 black patients in the New York sample received a project diagnosis of an affective illness not one had a hospital diagnosis of an affective illness of any kind.

CHAPTER XVII

SYMPTOM DIFFERENCES BETWEEN THE TWO SAMPLES

As in the Brooklyn–Netherne study, mean scores on the 45 sections of the Present State Examination were calculated for both the New York and London samples and the two compared, section by section. At the same time the distribution of scores on each of the 442 PSE items and 116 history items was calculated for both series and these also compared with one another, item by item. As before, this was done partly as a check on the consistency of the project diagnosis, and partly in an attempt to detect differences in symptoms either within or transcending traditional diagnostic categories.

The results of these comparisons are shown in TABLES 38, 39A and B, and 40. They are all difficult to interpret, for reasons which are clearly revealed by TABLE 39A. It was very much harder to interview patients in New York than in London, and because of this recorded levels of symptomatology are almost uniformly lower in New York patients. There were many reasons for this difficulty in obtaining reliable information from the New York patients, but the most important was probably the fact that 61 per cent of them, compared with only 28 per cent of the London patients, had been admitted to hospital against their wishes. As a result they were often angry and unco-operative, and not infrequently they denied or minimized their symptoms in the hope that this would secure their release. This situation is reflected by the judgemental ratings at the end of the PSE. 'Denies having psychiatric problems', 'overt hostility', 'deliberately misleading answers', 'credibility of patient's information doubted by interviewer', 'irritability', 'unconvincing denial of symptoms', and 'unclear or inadequate description of symptoms' were all rated significantly more often for the New York patients, frequently two or three times as often. Other factors also contributed to the problem. There were more patients lacking an adequate command of English in the New York sample (12 per cent v. 5 per cent) and more with little or no education. The fact that none of the project psychiatrists was a native of New York, or even of the United States, may also have increased communication difficulties somewhat (though it is important to appreciate that the project staff were not at any greater disadvantage in this respect than the majority of the hospitals' own medical staffs). The net result of all these factors was that the data from the mental state interview were rated as incomplete or unreliable for 39 per cent of the New York patients, compared with only 14 per cent in London. In addition, nearly half the New York patients had, by virtue of passing through a receiving hospital, been in hospital for over 5 days before being interviewed, and also a high proportion had recently received phenothiazine or hypnotic drugs, and both these factors would generally be expected to reduce their original levels of psychopathology.

TABLE 38

ALL 192 NEW YORK PATIENTS *V.* ALL 174 LONDON PATIENTS
PSE SECTION SCORES

I. MEAN SCORES SIGNIFICANTLY HIGHER IN THE LONDON PATIENTS

	NEW YORK	LONDON	p
Worry	3·20	5·18	0·001
General anxiety	1·97	3·24	0·001
Situational anxiety	0·19	1·01	0·001
Depression of mood	4·44	6·91	0·001
Loss of interests	1·08	1·66	0·001
Loss of concentration	0·95	1·62	0·001
Retardation	1·35	1·99	0·01
Loss of self-esteem	1·35	1·88	0·01
Depression O/E	0·87	1·43	0·01
Depersonalization	0·41	0·97	0·01
Subjective impairment of memory	0·51	0·86	0·01
Delusions of persecution	1·37	2·57	0·01
Religious delusions	0·20	0·55	0·01
Visual and other hallucinations	0·45	1·17	0·01
Obsessional symptoms	0·22	0·60	0·01
Slowed thought	2·30	2·94	0·02
Irritability	2·39	3·07	0·02
Delusions of reference	0·93	1·87	0·02
Tension	3·83	4·82	0·05
Ideas of reference	1·26	1·71	0·05
Perceptual disorders	0·30	0·61	0·05

2. MEAN SCORES SIGNIFICANTLY HIGHER IN THE NEW YORK PATIENTS

Ratings of 8	14·59	4·74	0·001

NOTE: Here and elsewhere the significance levels given for differences between mean section scores are derived from *t* tests.

As a consequence of these various influences not a single PSE section score or PSE symptom item (other than behavioural items) is significantly commoner in the New York sample than in the London sample. Instead, the New York patients show a threefold predominance of PSE ratings of 8—made either when the patient fails to answer, or when his reply is consistently ambiguous. The possibility was, of course, considered that at least part of this difference might be due to differences in rating threshold between the London and New York interviewers. Mean scores for the 45 sections of the

PSE were calculated for each rater, taking American and British patients separately where necessary, and a series of comparisons carried out, first among the four raters who had interviewed patients in each city, and then, for the two raters who had interviewed patients in both cities, between their ratings of their American and their English patients. The results showed that three of the six interviewers tended to rate lower (i.e. to have higher thresholds

TABLE 39A

ALL 192 NEW YORK PATIENTS *V.* ALL 174 LONDON PATIENTS. INDIVIDUAL PSE ITEMS SIGNIFICANTLY COMMONER IN THE NEW YORK PATIENTS

	NEW YORK	LONDON	*p*
Compulsory admission	117	49	0·001
In hospital more than 5 days before interview	89	8	0·001
Phenothiazine or butyrophenone drug in previous 24 hours	142	83	0·001
Sedative drug in previous 24 hours	36	13	0·01
Credibility of patient's information doubted by interviewer	43	16	0·01
Denies having psychiatric problems	68	38	0·05
Unclear or inadequate description of symptoms	100	66	0·05
Denial of ordinary worries	46	21	0·05
Deliberately misleading answers	13	3	0·05
Unconvincing denial of symptoms	27	9	0·05
BEHAVIOURAL RATINGS:			
Irritability	52	23	0·01
Anger or overt hostility	29	9	0·02
Idiosyncratic usage of ordinary words	12	2	0·05

Notes to this and the following Tables 39B to 44:
  1. The totals given are for all positive ratings combined.
  2. The significance levels given for differences between individual items are derived from chi-square tests (with Yates's modification).
  3. Occasionally items have been omitted, but only because they were very similar to other items which are included.

for the detection of psychopathology) than the others, but two of these had only been concerned with London patients and the one who had interviewed New York patients had only been responsible for 24 of them. Moreover, for both the psychiatrists who had interviewed patients in each city there was a big difference between the mean section scores of their English and their American patients, the latter scoring higher on section 25 (the total number of ratings of 8) but lower on nearly every other section. In other words, these inter-rater comparisons confirm that the differences in recorded levels of pathology between the two cities are not due to rater differences, and that

TABLE 39B

ALL 192 NEW YORK PATIENTS *V*. ALL 174 LONDON PATIENTS. INDIVIDUAL PSE ITEMS SIGNIFICANTLY COMMONER IN THE LONDON PATIENTS

	NEW YORK	LONDON	*p*
Severe or constant worrying	41	76	0·001
Restlessness	65	94	0·001
Subjective apprehensiveness	56	88	0·001
Autonomic anxiety attacks	48	73	0·001
Phobia of crowds	4	24	0·001
Phobia of social situations	2	17	0·001
Lack of energy	56	93	0·001
Future seems bleak or hopeless	54	88	0·001
Loss of all pleasure in life	45	88	0·001
Taking sleeping tablets (before admission)	35	65	0·001
Irritable with other people	43	78	0·001
Loss of enjoyment in everything	41	68	0·001
Inability to concentrate	45	87	0·001
Feeling of unreality	2	16	0·001
Delusions of persecution	26	53	0·001
General anxiety—overall rating	44	75	0·01
Phobia of enclosed spaces	4	21	0·01
Phobia of insects or heights	4	19	0·01
Thoughts seem to race through mind	30	55	0·01
Loss of self-confidence	48	72	0·01
Weeping	87	108	0·01
Thoughts of suicide	32	59	0·01
Depressive dreams	9	17	0·01
Unvarying depression	19	37	0·01
Compulsive rituals	0	10	0·01
Loss of interest in work	40	51	0·01
Loss of all previous interests	49	72	0·01
Depersonalization—overall rating	17	33	0·01
Delusions of reference	6	19	0·01
Religious delusions	7	21	0·01
Delusions of influence	11	27	0·01
Phobia of being alone	6	18	0·02
Sitting around doing nothing	48	68	0·02
Insomnia	95	109	0·02
Loss of libido	32	49	0·02
Annoyed by trivia	70	87	0·02
Obsessional symptoms—overall rating	13	27	0·02
Subjective impairment of memory	39	58	0·02
Subjective thought disorder—overall rating	10	23	0·02
Olfactory hallucinations	7	18	0·02
Fear of going insane	29	44	0·05
Muddled thinking	64	81	0·05
Ill at ease in company	45	58	0·05
Desire for solitude	56	71	0·05

TABLE 39B *(cont.)*

	NEW YORK	LONDON	p
Severe depression of mood	75	94	0·05
Premenstrual mood change	16	29	0·05
Hyperactivity—overall rating	15	28	0·05
Complaint of loss of emotions	17	29	0·05
Loss of insight	105	114	0·05
Conviction of ability to read other's thoughts	1	8	0·05
Suspicious of people's intentions	19	33	0·05
Depressive delusions—overall rating	7	16	0·05
Tactile hallucinations	4	12	0·05
Delusion of organization helping, not harming, the patient	2	11	0·05
BEHAVIOURAL RATINGS:			
Depressive mood—overall rating	58	91	0·001
Weeping	25	53	0·001
Anxiety—overall rating	41	62	0·01
Sad, mournful expression	56	73	0·02
Voice chokes with distress	10	21	0·05
Agitation—overall rating	31	46	0·05
Tachycardia	51	64	0·05

such rater differences as there are serve to reduce them rather than to accentuate them.

Because so many PSE items and section scores are significantly commoner in the London patients [see TABLES 38 and 39B] little significance can be attached to most of them. It is, however, symptoms of depression and anxiety which predominate most strongly, rather than schizophrenic or manic symptoms. In fact, several sections with schizophrenic implications (loss of insight, motor or postural abnormalities, auditory hallucinations, non-social speech, restriction of speech, verbal mannerisms, and incomprehensibility) are scored higher in the New York patients, not to a statistically significant extent, but perhaps worthy of note in view of the general tendency for all items to predominate in the London patients. The history items in TABLE 40 make it clear that addiction to alcohol and the psychotic states produced by alcohol are much commoner among the New York patients, and to a lesser extent drug addiction also. There is also a suggestion—but only a suggestion, because the relevant data were not derived from the whole sample—that although the two samples do not differ in the number of previous episodes of psychiatric illness, the number of hospital admissions, or the total time spent in hospital previously, the New York patients tended to have developed serious symptoms at an earlier age and to have remained incapacitated by them, while a higher proportion of the London patients developed florid symptoms shortly before admission. These differences may reflect a modest

TABLE 40

ALL 192 NEW YORK PATIENTS *V*. ALL 174 LONDON PATIENTS.
HISTORY ITEMS

I. ITEMS SIGNIFICANTLY COMMONER IN THE NEW YORK PATIENTS

	NEW YORK	LONDON	p
Excessive drinking in past month	51	9	0·001
Gets 'the shakes' after drinking	43	8	0·001
Evidence of dependence on alcohol in past year	47	8	0·001
Frank withdrawal symptoms in past	41	8	0·001
Alcoholism important reason for admission	47	7	0·001
Onset of heavy drinking over 5 years ago	45	9	0·001
Previous hospitalization for alcoholism	30	6	0·001
Serious psychiatric symptoms before 20[1]	33	22	0·001
Started using drugs over 5 years ago	11	1	0·01
Prolonged paranoid state while drinking	10	0	0·01
Prolonged hallucinosis while drinking	10	0	0·01
Serious communication difficulties	36	11	0·01
Drug abuse in last month	13	2	0·02
Psychiatric admission before 20[1]	23	17	0·02
Incapable of working before present episode[1]	17	13	0·02

2. ITEMS SIGNIFICANTLY COMMONER IN THE LONDON PATIENTS

	NEW YORK	LONDON	p
Admits having emotional symptoms or problems	54	110	0·001
Florid symptoms immediately before admission[1]	48	80	0·05

3. IMPORTANT ITEMS NOT DIFFERING SIGNIFICANTLY BETWEEN NEW YORK AND LONDON PATIENTS

Number of previous episodes of psychiatric illness[1]
Number of previous psychiatric admissions[1]
Total time in hospital previously[1]

[1] These comparisons are based only on the 103 New York patients and 163 London patients in whom this section of the history was completed.

predominance of chronic states in the New York sample—chronic schizophrenia or persistent personality disorder, with or without addiction to alcohol or drugs—and a predominance of acute illnesses, schizophrenic or affective, in the London sample.

As in the Brooklyn–Netherne study, these comparisons of the two samples were followed by analogous comparisons between the patients in each city with a project diagnosis of schizophrenia, and between those in each city with a project diagnosis of affective illness. Fifty-six (29 per cent) of the New York patients and 61 (35 per cent) of the London patients had a final project diagnosis of schizophrenia (categories 295·0–295·9 in ICD 8), and TABLES 41 and 42 show the significant differences between these two groups. In general the section scores and items which emerge are the same as those discussed previously in the comparison of the two parent populations. It is significant, though, that the symptoms predominating in the London patients are either affective symptoms or features of acute rather than chronic schizophrenic illnesses—they are mainly delusions or subjective experiences of disordered

TABLE 41

56 NEW YORK SCHIZOPHRENICS *V.* 61 LONDON SCHIZOPHRENICS.
PSE SECTION SCORES

1. MEAN SCORES SIGNIFICANTLY HIGHER IN THE NEW YORK PATIENTS

	NEW YORK	LONDON	p
Ratings of 8	21·16	6·61	0·001
Motor/postural abnormalities	1·04	0·39	0·01

2. MEAN SCORES SIGNIFICANTLY HIGHER IN THE LONDON PATIENTS

Delusions of persecution	3·20	6·10	0·01
Religious delusions	0·39	1·23	0·01
Situational anxiety	0·09	0·72	0·02
Perceptual disturbances	0·25	0·95	0·02
Delusions of reference	2·46	4·67	0·05
Visual and other hallucinations	0·89	2·15	0·05

thought, rather than blunting of affect, or idiosyncracies of speech or behaviour. One other difference is perhaps worth commenting on: the predominance of London patients with a delusional belief in an organization which, far from being malign, is actually helping them in some way. Paranoid delusions of all kinds are commoner in the London patients but this particular delusion stands out disproportionately. Possibly it is a reflection of different cultural attitudes to the authorities and organizations that impinge on people's everyday lives, the Londoner's concept of authority being coloured by the benevolent role of the Welfare State, and perhaps also by the popular image of the Metropolitan Police.

Sixty-two (32 per cent) of the New York patients and 76 (44 per cent) of the London patients had a final project diagnosis of some form of affective illness. (As before, all patients with a project diagnosis of affective psychosis (ICD categories 296·0–296·9), reactive depressive psychosis (ICD category 298·0), or depressive neurosis (ICD category 300·4) were included in this rubric.) The significant differences between the New York and London

TABLE 42

56 NEW YORK SCHIZOPHRENICS *V.* 61 LONDON SCHIZOPHRENICS.
INDIVIDUAL PSE ITEMS

1. ITEMS SIGNIFICANTLY COMMONER IN THE NEW YORK PATIENTS

	NEW YORK	LONDON	p
Compulsory admission	46	26	0·001
In hospital more than 5 days before interview	32	3	0·001
Phenothiazine or butyrophenone drug in previous 24 hours	142	83	0·001
Poor rapport between interviewer and patient	42	28	0·01
Credibility of patient's information doubted by interviewer	16	6	0·01
Worry about appearance	11	3	0·05
BEHAVIOURAL RATINGS:			
Anger or overt hostility	15	3	0·01
Irritability	18	7	0·05
Idiosyncratic usage of ordinary words	10	2	0·05

2. ITEMS SIGNIFICANTLY COMMONER IN THE LONDON PATIENTS

	NEW YORK	LONDON	p
Delusions of persecution	14	43	0·001
Worrying—overall rating	13	31	0·01
Delusion of organization helping, rather than harming, the patient	0	9	0·01
Religious delusions	4	17	0·01
Delusions of influence	10	25	0·02
Delusions of reference	15	35	0·02
Attacks of palpitations	6	19	0·02
Subjective thought disorder—overall rating	10	23	0·05
Thought broadcasting	10	22	0·05
Nocturnal anxiety attacks	3	12	0·05
Phobia of enclosed spaces	0	6	0·05
Phobia of social situations	0	6	0·05
Loss of former interests	9	21	0·05
Loss of enjoyment in everything	8	20	0·05
Irritable with other people	10	26	0·05

patients are shown in TABLES 43 and 44. Again, most of the items in these tables are ones that have appeared previously in the comparison of the two parent populations. Those predominating in the London patients are mainly indicative of anxiety or agitation rather than of retarded depression. This is a change from the analogous comparison in the Brooklyn–Netherne study where the English patients showed a marked predominance of the clinical features of classical manic-depressive depression [p. 77]. The change is explicable, though, in the light of the altered diagnostic composition of the affective populations. Whereas the proportion of the London affective group with manic-depressive illnesses of depressive type is much the same as in the Netherne series (41 per cent compared with 43 per cent), the corresponding proportion of the New York affective group is considerably higher than in the Brooklyn series (53 per cent compared with 36 per cent).

In summary, fruitful interpretation of these detailed item by item comparisons is impaired by the difference in the adequacy of the data for the two

TABLE 43

62 NEW YORK AFFECTIVES *V.* 76 LONDON AFFECTIVES.
PSE SECTION SCORES

1. MEAN SCORES SIGNIFICANTLY HIGHER IN THE NEW YORK PATIENTS

	NEW YORK	LONDON	*p*
Ratings of 8	14·16	4·17	0·001

2. MEAN SCORES SIGNIFICANTLY HIGHER IN THE LONDON PATIENTS

Depression O/E	1·42	2·18	0·001
Subjective memory impairment	0·44	1·01	0·001
Tension	4·82	6·93	0·01
Depressive mood	6·79	9·70	0·01
Impaired concentration	1·39	2·24	0·01
Depersonalization	0·42	1·20	0·01
General anxiety	2·39	3·95	0·02
Worry	4·89	6·62	0·05
Irritability	2·65	3·61	0·05
Loss of interests	1·65	2·28	0·05

samples of patients. It is clear, however, that the constellation of clinical features associated with alcoholism, and to a lesser extent with drug dependence, is much commoner in the New York patients, and that symptoms of anxiety and depression tend to be commoner in the London patients. There is also a suggestion that chronic disorders of personality and behaviour are rather commoner in the New York series, and acute florid illnesses, both schizophrenic and depressive, somewhat commoner in the London series. All these differences are compatible with the differences in the project diagnoses given to the two populations. There are far more alcoholics (23 per cent *v.* 5 per cent) in the New York sample than in the London sample, and also more drug addicts (3·1 per cent *v.* 0·6 per cent) and patients with personality disorders (4·2 per cent *v.* 2·9 per cent); on the other hand, there are more affectives (44 per cent *v.* 32 per cent), schizophrenics (35 per cent *v.* 29 per cent),

TABLE 44

62 NEW YORK AFFECTIVES *V.* 76 LONDON AFFECTIVES.
INDIVIDUAL PSE ITEMS

1. ITEMS SIGNIFICANTLY COMMONER IN THE NEW YORK PATIENTS

	NEW YORK	LONDON	p
Compulsory admission	33	17	0·001
Phenothiazine or butyrophenone drug in previous 24 hours	49	30	0·001
Unclear or inadequate description of symptoms	18	9	0·01
Denial of ordinary worries	12	4	0·05
Unconvincing denial of symptoms	9	2	0·05
Answers apparently at random	5	0	0·05

2. ITEMS SIGNIFICANTLY COMMONER IN THE LONDON PATIENTS

	NEW YORK	LONDON	p
Restlessness	22	54	0·001
Feeling that life is not worth living	20	51	0·001
Inability to concentrate	20	49	0·001
Thoughts seem to race through mind	9	36	0·001
Increased muscular tension	32	58	0·01
Subjective apprehensiveness	21	46	0·01
Autonomic anxiety attacks	17	40	0·01
Lack of energy	25	49	0·01
Future seems bleak or hopeless	21	45	0·01
Unvarying depression	10	29	0·01
Taking sleeping tablets (before admission)	18	41	0·01
Inability to name President/Prime Minister	1	13	0·01
Loss of enjoyment in everything	20	41	0·02
Difficulty relaxing	31	55	0·05
Pacing up and down	20	43	0·05
General anxiety—overall rating	15	40	0·05
Thoughts keep getting muddled	22	46	0·05
Irritability with others	24	44	0·05
Angry with self	5	33	0·05
Depersonalization	0	8	0·05
BEHAVIOURAL RATINGS:			
Weeping	10	32	0·05

and neurotics (4 per cent *v.* 1·6 per cent) in the London sample. The fact that these symptomatic and diagnostic differences match one another is evidence that the diagnostic criteria were reasonably consistent; and no major symptomatic differences have been detected either within the broad diagnostic groupings studied or running across them.

PART 4. CONCLUSIONS

CHAPTER XVIII

GENERAL DISCUSSION OF RESULTS

THE results of this comparison of samples of admissions to public mental hospitals in New York and London are essentially the same as, and so confirm, the results of the original single hospital study. When the same diagnostic criteria are used on both sides of the Atlantic patients with alcoholic disorders are significantly commoner in New York and patients with depressive illnesses significantly commoner in London, but for other diagnostic categories, including schizophrenia, the differences are trivial and statistically insignificant.

The significance of these findings hinges on the assumption that the diagnostic criteria used were indeed the same in both cities. The precautions taken to minimize diagnostic differences, and the studies carried out of the consistency of the diagnostic criteria of the project staff, have already been described, but in view of the critical importance of the issue it is necessary to raise the subject once more.

The Diagno diagnoses of the New York and London patients suggested that the project psychiatrists were using a rather broader concept of schizophrenia in London than in New York, and somewhat broader concepts of affective illness and alcoholism in New York than in London. A canonical variate analysis produced similar implications; namely, that the project criteria for a diagnosis of schizophrenia were broader in London than in New York, and the other way about for a diagnosis of affective psychosis. The crucial question is, are the inconsistencies suggested by these results sufficiently great to impair, or alter, the conclusions to be drawn from a comparison of the two sets of project diagnoses? The most direct way of answering this question is to replace the project diagnoses by the 'canonical variate diagnoses' shown in TABLE 29 and compare these. In fact, as TABLE 45 shows, no important change results. The difference between the proportions of patients diagnosed as schizophrenic in the two samples is still statistically insignificant; indeed it is reduced even further. The difference between the proportions of the two samples diagnosed as psychotic affective increases, but still does not reach statistical significance; and the difference between the proportions diagnosed as neurotic remains significant, as it was before. For reasons discussed previously these 'canonical variate diagnoses' are necessarily based on consistent criteria [p. 51]. This demonstration therefore confirms the statement made previously in CHAPTER XV that the inconsistencies in the diagnostic criteria of the project psychiatrists, though real, are trivial in comparison with the differences between the New York and London psychiatrists, and do not significantly affect the conclusions to be drawn from a comparison of the project diagnoses of the two samples of patients. The fact that the transatlantic differences revealed in the diagnostic criteria of the project staff are different in the New York–London and Brooklyn–Netherne comparisons, in spite of the fact that the identity of the psychiatrists concerned and the means by which project diagnoses were made were substantially the same in both, is a further indication that they reflect minor chance fluctuations rather than any systematic transatlantic bias.

TABLE 45

THE EFFECT OF REPLACING PROJECT DIAGNOSES BY
'CANONICAL VARIATE DIAGNOSES'

	PROJECT DIAGNOSES			CANONICAL VARIATE DIAGNOSES		
	NEW YORK		LONDON	NEW YORK		LONDON
	%		%	%		%
Schizophrenia	29	n.s.	35	30	n.s.	32
Affective						
psychoses	26	n.s.	29	21	n.s.	29
Neuroses	8	**	18	12	*	21

KEY: n.s. difference not significant
* difference significant at the 2 per cent level
** difference significant at the 1 per cent level

As in the Brooklyn–Netherne comparison, diagnostic differences that persist when hospital diagnoses are replaced by the uniform criteria of the project diagnosis and those which are eliminated by this means need to be discussed separately. The only persisting differences that are statistically significant are a higher proportion of patients in the New York sample with alcohol addiction, habitual excessive drinking, and alcoholic disorders as a whole, and a higher proportion in the London sample with depressive neuroses and affective illnesses as a whole. Once again it must be stressed that it is unwarranted to draw conclusions about the relative prevalence of these conditions in the two cities from these findings. Too small a proportion of the mentally ill are admitted to public mental hospitals, and social factors which vary from one setting to another exert too strong an influence on referral and admission policies. The higher proportion of London admissions with depressive illnesses might, for instance, be due simply to a selective loss of depressed patients in New York to reception hospitals, private hospitals, and psychiatrists in private office practice. The fivefold difference in the proportion of patients with alcoholic disorders (23 per cent in New York v.

5 per cent in London) is more impressive and may well reflect a genuine difference in the prevalence of alcoholism in the two cities, but the over-representation of lower social classes in the New York sample and the peculiar vulnerability of alcoholics to the vagaries of hospital admission policies mean that only the most tentative conclusions can be drawn even from a difference of this magnitude.

It may be recalled that the original Brooklyn–Netherne comparison also revealed a significantly higher proportion of British patients with depressive psychoses, particularly typical manic-depressive illness, and a higher proportion with anxiety neuroses. These differences did not emerge in this second study and it is not clear why this was so, for the predominance of Netherne patients with typical manic-depressive depressions was one of the most prominent findings of that study. The proportion of patients with project diagnoses of affective or neurotic illness was lower in the London series than it had been at Netherne, but exactly the same change took place between Brooklyn and New York. In fact, the most important change seems to have been that, whereas the proportion of the London affective patients with manic-depressive depressions was much the same as at Netherne (41 per cent compared with 43 per cent) the corresponding proportion of New York patients with manic-depressive depressions was considerably higher (53 per cent compared with 36 per cent). But why this should have been so is still unclear.

The most important conclusions to be drawn from this study are derived from those differences between the two sets of hospital diagnoses which were eliminated by the uniform criterion of the project diagnosis, rather than from those which remained. The differences between the hospital diagnoses of the New York and London samples were very prominent, with striking contrasts for nearly every major diagnostic category. There were six times as many alcoholics and twice as many schizophrenics in the New York sample, but twelve times as many manics and five times as many depressives in the London sample, and so on. When hospital diagnoses were replaced by project diagnoses, however, these differences were all either eliminated or reduced and the only ones to remain statistically significant were for alcoholic disorders, which remained five times as common in New York, and depressions, which remained half as common again in London.

The implication of this is, of course, that there are several major differences between the diagnostic criteria used by the staffs of the two groups of hospitals, and it is apparent from the previous discussion of the data shown in TABLES 33, 34, 36, and 37 that the general pattern of these differences is much the same as in the earlier Brooklyn–Netherne comparison. As TABLE 36 shows, the degree of agreement or disagreement between the New York hospital psychiatrists and the project psychiatrists varies greatly from one diagnostic category to another. For alcoholism agreement is quite good. Both groups diagnosed about 20 per cent of the sample as having an alcoholic disorder and 32 of the 38 patients labelled as alcoholics by the hospital staff received the same diagnosis from the project staff. For mania, on the other hand, disagreement is total. Not one of the 11 patients receiving this diagnosis from the project staff was regarded as manic-depressive by the hospital staff, who instead diagnosed all but one of them as schizophrenics. (Ironically, the only patient in the whole series to receive a hospital diagnosis of mania had a project diagnosis of depression!) This agreement for alcoholism and disagreement over mania is just what was found in the Brooklyn–Netherne study. So too is the contrast between the overall patterns of diagnostic usage of the New York and London psychiatrists. Only 34 per cent of the London patients had hospital diagnoses of schizophrenia and the remaining non-organic patients were spread over at least four other diagnostic groupings—depressive psychoses (24 per cent), mania (7 per cent), neurotic illnesses (14 per cent), and personality disorders (5 per cent). By comparison, 61 per cent of the New York patients had hospital diagnoses of schizophrenia and only two other non-organic diagnoses were used with any frequency—depressive psychoses (5 per cent) and neurotic illness (4 per cent). Indeed, 82 per cent of the 144 patients in the New York sample with functional disorders (i.e. omitting alcoholics, and those with organic illnesses) received hospital diagnoses of schizophrenia, including 63 per cent of those with a project diagnosis of depressive psychosis, 91 per cent of those with a project diagnosis of mania, 69 per cent of those with a project diagnosis of neurosis, and 63 per cent of those with a project diagnosis of personality disorder.

It was suggested, while discussing the results of the Brooklyn–Netherne comparison, that the Brooklyn staff appeared to be ignoring the traditional symptomatic and prognostic implications of a diagnosis of schizophrenia and using the term so freely that it was in some danger of becoming a synonym for functional mental illness. Although the neglect of other diagnostic categories is not quite so extreme in this sample of patients, the general pattern is very similar and the same comments are appropriate. The situation is graphically illustrated by an analysis of the relationship between hospital diagnoses and symptoms reported previously by Gurland, Fleiss, Cooper, Sharpe, Kendell, and Roberts (1970). Seven different symptom profiles were defined and the hospital diagnoses of patients with each of these profiles examined. Among the London patients there was a clear relationship between symptom profile and diagnosis, but among the New York patients there was no significant relationship between the two, largely because the majority of patients were diagnosed as schizophrenics regardless of their symptomatology.

At the time, in 1966, when the studies described in this volume were first embarked upon it was known, or at least widely suspected, that there were differences in diagnostic usage between Britain and the United States. It was, in fact, our original expectation that part of the difference between the diagnostic statistics of English and American mental hospitals would prove to be due simply to differences in usage, but that a considerable part would prove to be due to genuine differences in the symptoms of patients entering hospital in the two countries. Indeed, we had envisaged spending much of our time studying the social and cultural correlates of these 'genuine' differences. Perhaps we should have been warned by the demonstration of Fletcher and his colleagues (Fletcher, Jones, Burrows, and Niden, 1964) that the large reported Anglo-American differences in the incidence of chronic bronchitis and emphysema were simply due to the fact that what was called emphysema in Chicago was called chronic bronchitis in London. At all events, our expectations were not fulfilled. Transatlantic differences in usage proved to be much more extensive and serious than had been foreseen and the remaining 'genuine' symptomatic differences to be correspondingly less impressive. As it slowly became clear that the diagnostic differences we had set out to elucidate were being generated by psychiatrists rather than by patients we changed our plans and shifted the main focus of our investigation away from the patients and onto the psychiatrists.

In essence, the comparisons of series of hospital admissions described here constitute a strategy in which the psychiatrist is held constant, by using a 'standard' project psychiatrist, and the patients varied, by examining series of both American and British patients. The alternative, or complementary, strategy is to hold the patient constant, by using only a single group of patients, and to vary the psychiatrists, by asking many different psychiatrists, American and British, to provide diagnoses for these selected patients. This alternative strategy was adopted by making videotapes of diagnostic interviews with a small number of patients, and then showing these to large audiences of psychiatrists both in the United States and in various parts of the British Isles and comparing the diagnoses made by the two. The results of these videotape comparisons have already been reported elsewhere (Kendell, Cooper, Gourlay, Copeland, Sharpe, and Gurland, 1971) but they can be usefully summarized here.

Videotapes were made of diagnostic interviews, lasting between 20 and 50 minutes, with eight patients, five of them English and three American. Between them they covered a wide range of symptomatology, though some were picked as 'typical' cases and others deliberately chosen in the expectation that they might give rise to diagnostic disagreement. These eight tapes were shown over the course of many months to several audiences of psychiatrists on both sides of the Atlantic. The psychiatrists seeing them were required to make detailed ratings of the symptoms they detected in each patient, and also to make a diagnosis, using the nomenclature of the *International Classification of Diseases*. Eventually, each tape was rated in this way by between 30 and 200 psychiatrists in each country and altogether over 700 psychiatrists were involved. In the British Isles a geographically representative sample was obtained for three of the tapes by holding a series of meetings in different regions—two in London, two in Scotland, two in Ireland and one each in Birmingham and Manchester. In the United States it was harder, for a variety of reasons, to obtain a similarly representative sample and most of the raters whose diagnoses are quoted here worked in the New York area, many of them on the staffs of State hospitals.

For the three patients whose symptoms were fairly typical of classical stereotypes there was substantial agreement between American and British raters, at least for the major category of illness involved. For three other patients with a mixture of schizophrenic and affective symptoms the majority of both American and British raters diagnosed schizophrenia, but for all three a substantial minority of British raters (20 per cent to 34 per cent) diagnosed an affective psychosis instead. For the two remaining patients there was really serious disagreement, with most British raters diagnosing either a personality disorder or a neurotic illness but the majority of the Americans again diagnosing schizophrenia. In fact, seven of the eight patients were regarded as schizophrenics by over two-thirds of the American raters. There was also a remarkable tendency for American psychiatrists to perceive more pathology than British psychiatrists. This was particularly striking for symptoms with strong schizophrenic connotations, but it applied to some extent to the entire range of symptoms and to all eight patients.

In general, the results of these videotape studies confirm and amplify those of the earlier hospital admission comparisons. Both indicate that the concept of schizophrenia held by psychiatrists in the New York area is much broader than that held by London psychiatrists and embraces substantial parts of what the latter would regard as depressive illness, neurotic illness or personality disorder, and almost the whole of what would be regarded in London as mania. The contrast between the two concepts is illustrated graphically in FIGURE 5.

In a situation such as this, where two large groups of experienced psychiatrists disagree profoundly about how one of their major diagnostic terms should be used, the temptation to ask who is right is a strong one. It is important to realize, though, that in our present state of knowledge such a question is not only unanswerable, it is inherently meaningless. Schizophrenia, like all other varieties of functional mental illness recognized in our nomenclature, is defined in terms of its clinical picture. In Scadding's terminology, its defining characteristic is its syndrome, and so the decision whether or not an individual patient has schizophrenia can only be made by the 'Hippocratic procedure' of comparing the patient's symptoms with those of the illness and deciding whether the resemblance is adequate (Scadding, 1967). If two groups of psychiatrists habitually disagree about whether patients of a particular kind do or do not have schizophrenia all one can say is that they are using the word in different ways. One may discuss whose concept is more useful, or whose is closer to Bleuler's original concept, but one cannot meaningfully discuss who is right, for we have no external criterion to appeal to—no morbid anatomy, no aetiological agent, no biochemical or physiological anomaly.

Having said this, however, it does seem, at least to the authors of this volume, that the New York concept of schizophrenia is not a useful one and is likely to inhibit fruitful research if it is widely adopted. We say this largely because the concept has, through the accretion of subsidiary concepts like schizo-affective schizophrenia and pseudoneurotic schizophrenia (Hoch and Polatin, 1949) become so all-embracing that it is close to becoming a synonym for functional mental illness, a sort of twentieth-century reincarnation of Zeller's *Einheitspsychose*. Indeed, some American authors have said frankly

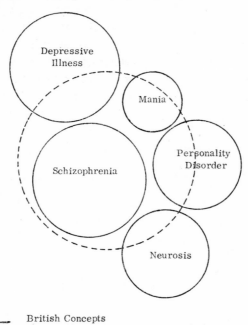

_____ British Concepts

_ _ _ _ _ New York Concept of Schizophrenia

FIG. 5. The difference between the New York and British concepts
of schizophrenia.

that they regard schizophrenia simply as a term denoting the more severe forms of a single mental illness (Menninger, 1963; Weinstock, 1968). If, however, we were all to concur with this usage we would in effect be abandoning all attempt at classification of non-organic illness. And in doing this we would inevitably lose sight of important relationships between patterns of symptoms and outcome and response to treatment, and thus all hope of identifying the more fundamental differences underlying these therapeutic and prognostic relationships.

It is established, both by the hospital admission comparisons and the videotape studies, that there is a striking difference between the diagnostic habits of psychiatrists in London and New York, but the significance of this difference depends very much on the extent to which it is indicative of differences between American and British psychiatry as a whole. We have quite good evidence from a videotape comparison described in detail elsewhere (Copeland, Cooper, Kendell, and Gourlay, 1971) that there is little variation in diagnostic usage from one region to another within the British Isles. In this study three of the videotapes referred to above were shown to audiences of psychiatrists in London and in six different regional centres in other parts of the British Isles. The diagnoses of psychiatrists trained in Glasgow differed from those of their colleagues elsewhere on one of the tapes, but this was the only significant diagnostic difference to emerge; in particular, the diagnoses of London-trained psychiatrists did not differ from those of British psychiatrists as a whole on any of the three tapes. We do not yet know, however, to what extent New York psychiatrists are representative of American psychiatry, for so far no comparable study has been carried out comparing the diagnostic behaviour of psychiatrists in different centres within the United States. The 450 American psychiatrists involved in the videotape studies referred to earlier were mostly drawn from the staffs of the New York Psychiatric Institute and other State, city and private hospitals supplying the New York metropolitan area. Some were from Boston, Baltimore, or New Jersey, but the sample was still derived almost entirely from the Eastern seaboard.

There are, in fact, a number of indications that New York psychiatrists do have a significantly broader concept of schizophrenia than other American psychiatrists. Kramer, Pollack, and Redick (1961) showed that in 1950 the age-adjusted first-admission rate for schizophrenia in New York State had risen considerably since 1940 and was higher than in any other State in the entire country. Some further equally suggestive figures of more recent origin are shown in TABLE 46. For the United States as a whole 18 per cent of all admissions to public mental hospitals are diagnosed as schizophrenics, or 31 per cent of all admissions other than organic brain syndromes and addictive states (alcohol and drugs). For California and Illinois, two large States of similar size and population distribution to New York State, the corresponding proportions are similar. For New York State, though, they are considerably higher—25 per cent and 52 per cent—and similar differences exist between the corresponding first-admission rates for schizophrenia. These differences might, of course, be due to a higher prevalence of schizophrenia in New York, or to a lack of alternative treatment facilities, but they certainly raise the possibility that schizophrenia is diagnosed more readily in New York than elsewhere. (Incidentally, the corresponding figures for North Carolina, which are lower than those for the United States as a whole, suggest that North Carolina psychiatrists have a rather more restricted concept of schizo-phrenia than most other Americans, which may help to explain why Sandifer and his colleagues found no difference in the proportion of patients regarded as schizophrenic by his American and British raters (Sandifer, Hordern, Timbury, and Green, 1968).)

Preliminary videotape comparisons between New York and other centres on the Pacific coast and in the Mid-west indicate that New York psychiatrists do indeed have a wider concept of schizophrenia than other American psychiatrists. It is probably also significant that several of the ideas that have been instrumental in enlarging the American concept of schizophrenia, like the introduction of the concept of pseudoneurotic schizophrenia (Hoch and Polatin, 1949) and the dictum that 'even a trace of schizophrenia is schizophrenia' (Lewis and Piotrowski, 1954), originated in the New York State Psychiatric Institute and so can be expected to have been more influential in New York than elsewhere.

TABLE 46

THE VARIATION BETWEEN STATES IN THE PROPORTION OF FIRST ADMISSIONS TO PUBLIC MENTAL HOSPITALS DIAGNOSED AS SCHIZOPHRENICS, AND THE CORRESPONDING FIRST-ADMISSION RATES FOR SCHIZOPHRENIA

	THE UNITED STATES AS A WHOLE	NEW YORK STATE	ILLINOIS	CALI-FORNIA	NORTH CAROLINA
Schizophrenia as a proportion of all first admissions	17·9%	24·8%	19·3%	19·1%	9·0%
As above—excluding organic brain syndromes and addictions	30·9%	51·7%	34·3%	29·7%	16·2%
First-admission rate for schizophrenia per 100,000 population[1]	15·6	36·0	14·1	13·1	11·8

Calculated from data in the National Institute of Mental Health's *Reference Tables on Patients in Mental Health Facilities* for 1968, and from data supplied by Dr. Morton Kramer (Chief, Biometry Branch, NIMH).

[1] Age-adjusted to the 1960 United States population.

It may well be, therefore, that the contrast revealed here between New York and London psychiatrists is giving a misleadingly alarming picture of overall Anglo-American differences, and that further studies within the United States will show that New York is not typical of the country as a whole. However, the evidence already available makes it almost inconceivable that the diagnostic differences between 'typical' American and British psychiatrists could prove to be anything other than substantial. The differences in national statistics reviewed by Kramer (1969a) are too great, involving nine- and tenfold differences in first-admission rates for some diagnostic categories; and there is also the evidence of previous Anglo-American videotape comparisons based on the diagnoses of psychiatrists from other parts of the United States (Sandifer, Hordern, Timbury, and Green, 1968; Katz,

Cole, and Lowery, 1969). In any case, it must be realized that, even if the diagnostic predilections of New York psychiatrists were shown to be atypical of American psychiatry as a whole, and the extent of Anglo-American disagreement reduced thereby, this would create an equally serious discrepancy between the thousands of psychiatrists in New York and their colleagues elsewhere. The magnitude of the diagnostic disparity would not be affected, only its geographical location—within the United States, rather than between the United States and Britain.

At present it is unclear which aspects of the diagnostic process are involved in the differences in usage we have demonstrated, or how these differences arose historically. The most obvious explanation is simply that American and British psychiatrists define diagnostic terms like schizophrenia and manic-depressive illness in different ways, but the available evidence suggests that this is, at best, only a partial explanation. Hordern, Sandifer, Green, and Timbury (1968) asked small groups of psychiatrists in North Carolina, London, and Glasgow to list in order of importance the typical symptoms of 20 of the most commonly used diagnostic categories, and found that the differences between the American and British groups were small and no greater than those between the individual members of each group on its own, in spite of the fact that they had previously demonstrated substantial cross-national differences in actual diagnostic usage among these same psychiatrists. As was suggested above, North Carolina psychiatrists are probably closer to British psychiatrists than their counterparts in most other American centres in their use of the key diagnosis of schizophrenia, but even so these findings suggest that the main cause of the Anglo-American diagnostic differences revealed here must be sought elsewhere.

Three other possibilities suggest themselves. First, the apparent similarity between American and British diagnostic stereotypes may be illusory, because the diagnoses in question are defined by technical terms which may themselves hold different meanings in the two countries. American and British psychiatrists may agree, for example, that schizophrenia is characterized by thought disorder and flattening of affect, but mean different things by flattening of affect and thought disorder. Secondly, disagreement may occur because one group insists on a much closer correspondence than the other between the symptoms of the patient and those of the stereotype before being prepared to accept the diagnosis as established. Thirdly, the two may actually perceive, or recognize, different abnormalities in spite of observing exactly the same samples of behaviour. Perhaps the most likely explanation is that there are significant differences between American and British psychiatrists at each of these levels and that the observed differences in usage are the cumulative product of all three.

The videotape comparisons whose results were summarized above provide many examples of what appear to be perceptual differences between American and British raters. Both we and Katz found significant differences between the ratings of American and British psychiatrists on Lorr's In-Patient Multi-dimensional Psychiatric Scale (Lorr and Klett, 1967), although all technical terms are carefully avoided in this instrument and its ratings are straight-forward measures of deviation from normal behaviour on linear scales. In spite of this, it has been an invariable finding that American psychiatrists rate higher, on both American and English patients, in all areas of psycho-pathology, particularly in those with strong schizophrenic connotations. When ratings involving technical terms are compared, however, much larger differences are obtained. The subject of one videotaped interview, for instance, was rated by 67 per cent of a group of 133 American psychiatrists as having delusions, by 63 per cent as having passivity feelings, and by 58 per cent as showing thought disorder. The corresponding percentages for an audience of 194 British psychiatrists shown the same videotape were 12 per cent for delusions, 8 per cent for passivity feelings, and 5 per cent for thought dis-order. The fact that these discrepancies are so much larger than those between the same psychiatrists' IMPS ratings strongly suggests that an important conceptual element is present on top of the perceptual difference; it suggests, in other words, that the two groups mean different things by thought dis-order and passivity feelings as well as perceiving or recognizing different deviations from normal behaviour to begin with.

Although we have no direct evidence on the point it is likely also that there are important differences between American and British psychiatrists in the degree of similarity between the patient's symptoms and those of the diag-nostic stereotype regarded as necessary to establish particular diagnoses. Because many patients do not fit neatly into well-defined diagnostic categories every classification has to have, in practice if not in theory, at least one category which is only loosely defined and can act as a 'rag bag' for patients who do not fit in elsewhere. The dictum that 'even a trace of schizophrenia is schizophrenia' promulgated by Nolan Lewis at the New York State Psychiatric Institute (Lewis and Piotrowski, 1954) obviously lays the ground for a very loose definition of schizophrenia, enabling it to be used as a handy label for patients who do not possess the classical features of any other stereotype. It is our impression that patients with nondescript symptoms tend to be diagnosed as schizophrenics by New York psychiatrists at least in part because other diagnoses like manic-depressive illness are ruled out by the very close correspondence they require between the patients' symptoms and those of this stereotype before the diagnosis can be made. In Britain, on the other hand, the situation tends to be the other way about. Quite close agreement is often insisted upon between the patient's symptoms and those of the stereotype for a diagnosis of schizophrenia, but much greater latitude is allowed for a diagnosis of depressive illness. Although no one has gone so far as to claim that 'even a trace of depression is depression', mood disturb-ances are ubiquitous and provide a convenient pretext for allocating many poorly defined illnesses to the affective rubric.

The disparity between American and British diagnostic concepts raises another issue of much greater importance than the question of whose diagnoses are the more useful. Diagnoses are the most important of all our technical terms because they are the means by which we identify the subject-matter of most of our research. They are the labels by which we identify the patients whose amine metabolism we were studying, or who received the new drug whose efficacy we were testing. If these crucial terms are used in widely differing ways by different groups of psychiatrists communication between them will be gravely hindered. Indeed, the large differences between American and British diagnostic usage revealed here imply that rather different interpretations must now be placed by British psychiatrists on much recent American research on schizophrenia, and by American psychiatrists on several British studies of affective disorders. The significance to British psychiatrists of, for example, Lidz's studies of the families of schizophrenics (Lidz, Fleck, and Cornelison, 1965) and the aetiological theories derived from these, must be affected by the suspicion that they themselves would not have regarded many of his cases as schizophrenics in the first place. Similarly, American psychiatrists may well need to revise their assessment of several British studies of depressions, on the grounds that many of the patients involved were not in fact suffering from depressive illnesses in the sense in which they understand the term. If, subsequently, serious differences in diagnostic usage are found within different centres in the United States the situation will become even more chaotic. Psychiatrists in New York will have to disregard, or be misled by, the work of Winokur and his colleagues in St. Louis on manic-depressive illness (Winokur, Clayton, and Reich, 1969), and they in turn will have to do the same for Kallmann's genetic studies (Kallmann, 1946), and so on. This is, of course, speculative and perhaps unnecessarily pessimistic, but it does serve to underline our dependence on a reasonable uniformity of diagnostic usage in our interpretation of all research conducted outside the walls of our own institutes. Much clinical and biological research can be partly shielded from the consequences of discrepant diagnostic criteria by restricting the case material to subjects with very typical symptoms, but in epidemiological work this is impossible and for this reason findings in large parts of this field may have to be qualified by uncertainty about the diagnostic criteria employed.

This disastrous effect of differences in diagnostic concepts on communication overshadows all the other consequences—the creation of spurious disparities in prevalence and admission rates, misguided arguments about which illness the patient is 'really' suffering from, and so on. It is a sobering thought, too, that the gross differences revealed here between New York and London have arisen in spite of the advantages of a common language and many shared cultural values. At present we do not know whether similar disparities are to be found between the diagnoses made by, say, French and Russian psychiatrists, but the opportunities for mutual misunderstanding must be greatly increased by language differences. A pilot study conducted by the World Health Organization a few years ago (Shepherd, Brooke, Cooper, and Lin, 1968) found that the level of disagreement among a small group of eminent psychiatrists from eight countries in different parts of the world was no greater than that within a group of British psychiatrists, but it would be unwise to read too much into this finding. The part of the study concerned with diagnosis was based mainly on written case-histories, rather than videotapes or film, and so disagreements about the presence or absence of diagnostically crucial features like thought disorder or blunting of affect were eliminated. And most of the psychiatrists involved were experienced international travellers whose diagnoses cannot safely be assumed to reflect those their more sheltered colleagues might have made.

The findings of these studies raise the question of whether the diagnostic component of mental hospital statistics is of any value, other than locally within individual hospitals. At present, international comparisons would obviously be more misleading than helpful, and even within the two countries concerned here wide variations between regions can be found which now seem likely to have a large iatrogenic component. Differences in the admission rates for schizophrenia between regions in the United States have already been commented upon [see TABLE 46], and even within the greater general uniformity demonstrated among British psychiatrists, it is possible to find similar differences if admission rates are examined at the level of individual hospitals. For instance, in 1964, for one hospital in north-west London 16 per cent of admissions were diagnosed as schizophrenics, and 49 per cent as having some type of affective disorder, whereas for another hospital with a similar suburban catchment area in south-east London the corresponding percentages were 27 per cent and 28 per cent. These local differences could well be due to the diagnostic eccentricities of only one or two psychiatrists.

In addition to differences in the diagnostic habits of psychiatrists, another factor encountered in the London hospitals involved in this study was uncertainty about exactly who made the hospital diagnosis, and when. There was no generally accepted procedure stipulating whose responsibility it was to make the official diagnosis, and when this was to be done. Indeed, we had the strong impression that in some instances, when the time came for the official returns to be sent in, the diagnosis was sometimes provided by a nurse or a member of the administrative staff. In addition many clinicians ignored the official request to use the nomenclature of the *International Classification of Diseases*, and recorded their own personal terms; these were sometimes easily translatable into ICD diagnoses, but labels such as '?suicide', 'hallucinatory state' or '?psychosis' were also encountered. It is worth considering how this unsatisfactory state of affairs could be improved.

A good deal of variation produced by differences between psychiatrists will always remain in ordinary hospital diagnosis, for administrative rules will have no effect upon their perception of their patients, or the meanings they attach to the terms they use. Such variations could, however, be mini-mized by the use of an agreed glossary of terms. If, in addition, there was general agreement among hospital psychiatrists to observe a few simple procedural rules, many of the major defects of the present haphazard system could be remedied. The following suggestions could be applied to both the United States and the United Kingdom:

1. The official admission diagnosis should be the responsibility of the most senior psychiatrist to have dealt clinically with the patient.

2. He should make this diagnosis, preferably in consultation with any other psychiatrists who had seen the patient, within a stated time of admission, perhaps 2 weeks, and it should be his responsibility to see that the diagnosis was properly recorded and coded on the appropriate form.

3. This official diagnosis should be restricted to the nomenclature of the current edition of the *International Classification of Diseases* (ICD) and the choice of term should be guided by the recommendations and definitions in the international glossary produced by the WHO (or, until this is available, the appropriate national glossary).

If these rules were observed, it is likely that, at least within regions or within countries, diagnostic practice in the recording of official statistics would become much more uniform. But this assumption would have to be tested, and one way of doing this would be to institute these measures in a number of hospitals specially selected for their statistical differences, and then to mount a special investigation in which the improved system would be compared, over a series of admissions, with the diagnoses of trained investigators using standardized interviewing and diagnostic procedures. The results of such an investigation would indicate whether it would be justified to make the major effort necessary to persuade all mental hospitals to adopt these rules of diagnostic procedure.

If the whole routine diagnostic system could be improved significantly, then hospitals or regions which still gave rise to unusual statistics would be worthy of special investigations to identify the sources of their uniqueness. Areas in which major alterations in psychiatric services were taking place could be expected to show changes in the distribution of different types of patients across the different components of the service, and these changes might indicate particular problems worthy of more detailed study. Probably the most that can be expected of a large-scale routine diagnostic system is that it should be capable of drawing attention to areas and problems worthy of more controlled and detailed investigation. These are all matters of psychi-atric interest and the responsibility for these improvements must be taken by psychiatrists, rather than by administrators as has happened too often in the past.

As the concept develops of an integrated system of psychiatric services serving a defined area and population, it becomes possible to envisage studies of the incidence and prevalence of psychiatric disorder through the use of cumulative case-registers. For such ventures, reliable methods of case-finding, and of the description and recording of diagnoses, become increasingly necessary, and it is perhaps from this direction that the greatest stimulus will come for further development of methods of collecting and recording diagnoses reliably on a large scale.

Like most research, the studies described in this monograph have produced only a partial solution to the questions the Diagnostic Project originally set out to answer, and have raised other questions in the process. Reduced to their simplest terms, the original questions were these: are the reported differences between the diagnostic statistics of American and British mental hospitals due to genuine differences in the symptoms of patients entering hospital in the two countries, or are they due to differences in diagnostic criteria on the two sides of the Atlantic; and, if they are genuine, do they reflect real differences in prevalence between the two countries, or merely nosocomial factors? To the first of these questions we have given a confident but incomplete answer. We have demonstrated that, within the age range studied, the reported differences between the diagnostic statistics of New York and London hospitals are largely, though not entirely, attributable to differences in the diagnostic criteria used in the two cities. We have also been able to demonstrate that the diagnostic criteria of London psychiatrists are fairly representative of those of British psychiatry as a whole. This is only a partial answer, for two reasons—we do not yet know to what extent New York psychiatrists are representative of the United States as a whole, and indeed have reasons for suspecting that they may not be very typical; and we can draw no conclusions about patients over the age of 60 because our studies have all been restricted to patients below this age. To the second question, concerning differences in prevalence, we cannot yet give any answer at all, because so far we have only studied hospital populations.

The current work and future intentions of the staff of the Diagnostic Project are based on this assessment of what has been accomplished so far, and are concerned in the first instance with filling the obvious gaps in the picture. It is clearly important to establish to what extent the diagnostic criteria employed by New York psychiatrists are typical of other American psychiatrists, and to what extent and in which areas they are not. With this aim in view the videotaped diagnostic interviews that have already been rated by audiences in New York and other centres on the Eastern seaboard are now being shown to groups of psychiatrists in other parts of the United States. Before long these comparisons can be expected to make at least the main features of any regional differences that may exist within the United States fairly clear, particularly if other workers also take an interest in this field now that a potentially serious problem has been identified.

The other outstanding need is to find out whether similar differences in diagnostic usage to those found here in the third to sixth decades of life also exist in other age ranges where the spectrum of illness is different. Kramer (1961) found Anglo-American differences in the admission rates of elderly patients just as striking as those involving the younger adults studied here. He found, for instance, that for psychosis with cerebral arteriosclerosis the admission rate per 100,000 population was 10 times higher in the United States than in England and Wales, in spite of a lower overall admission rate for elderly patients. In view of the considerable differences that have already been revealed between American and British diagnostic criteria it is likely that this disparity will also prove to be generated for the most part by psychiatrists rather than by patients. This cannot be assumed without being demonstrated, though, and a comparison of hospital admissions over the age of 60 in New York and London, analogous to that described here for younger patients, is currently under way. This time, however, the situation will be different in one important respect, for cerebral arteriosclerosis and the other organic states of the senium have a fairly clear-cut prognosis and are defined not by their syndromes but by their morbid anatomy; so in this comparison appropriate follow-up studies will generally be capable of resolving diagnostic disagreements one way or the other.

Once these two problems have been disposed of it is planned to tackle the second and more fundamental question of whether, underlying all these differences in hospital admission rates, there are genuine differences in the prevalence of some forms of mental illness between New York and London. This question has loomed unanswered in the background of both the studies that have been described, and it needs answering. In recent years many comparisons have been drawn between the prevalence figures for particular types of mental illness in different countries, and numerous interpretations have been placed on the cross-cultural differences which these reveal. But all these comparisons are subject to the assumption that the general methodology and diagnostic criteria employed were more or less the same in all the countries concerned. The gross differences revealed here between the diagnostic criteria of two groups of contemporary English-speaking psychiatrists make it clear that this assumption is a dangerous one, and underline the need for prevalence comparisons to be designed as such from the beginning, with a single research team operating in both countries and using exactly the same methods and diagnostic criteria in each. With the partial exception of Leighton's Stirling County and Yoruba comparison (Leighton, Lambo, Hughes, Leighton, Murphy, and Macklin, 1963) no such study has ever been done and the practical problems involved are certainly considerable. Potentially, however, cross-cultural epidemiological comparisons could be a very powerful means both of testing hypotheses relating different forms of mental illness to social and cultural variables, and of generating new hypotheses in the same area.

In many ways London and New York would be an ideal pair of 'cultures' to compare. Both have sufficiently well-developed psychiatric services to make an accurate prevalence estimate feasible; they are sufficiently similar in most of their social characteristics not to pose too many methodological difficulties, and yet they differ sharply in several important ways—in the incidence of other forms of deviant behaviour, in social attitudes to self-assertive and aggressive behaviour, in the distribution of wealth and social attitudes to wealth, and in religious and ethnic composition. Five or 10 years ago many psychiatrists would have been prepared to forecast the broad results of such a comparison with some confidence but, ironically, the hospital admission comparisons described here have undermined the basis of that confidence. But whether or not depressive illnesses proved to be commoner in London and schizophrenia to be commoner in New York, the results would be of great interest and would hold implications for most of our current aetiological theories, social, psychological, and genetic.

CHAPTER XIX

SUMMARY

THERE are large and persistent differences between the diagnostic statistics generated by American and British psychiatric hospitals. Although overall admission rates are similar in the two countries the admission rates for schizophrenia and arteriosclerotic dementia are considerably higher in the United States and the admission rate for manic-depressive illness higher in England and Wales; a detailed analysis of these differences by Kramer (1961) showed that in some age/sex categories ten- or even twentyfold differences are involved. These differences could be due to genuine differences in the clinical characteristics of patients entering hospital in the two countries, or to differences in the diagnostic criteria used by American and British psychiatrists, or to a combination of the two. And in so far as they are due to differences in the patients they might be the result either of real differences in prevalence between the two countries, or of differences in the availability and utilization of other treatment facilities.

The US–UK Diagnostic Project was created primarily in order to find out which of these possibilities was contributing, and in what ways, to the observed differences in mental hospital admission rates, and two complementary research teams, one based in New York and the other in London, were set up for this purpose.

The first study to be undertaken by the project, described in Part 2, was a comparison between a series of admissions to an English area mental hospital and an analogous series of admissions to an American State hospital, and was designed to measure how much of the difference between the normal hospital diagnoses of the two sets of patients would be eliminated when exactly the same diagnostic criteria were used on both sides of the Atlantic. The two hospitals concerned—the Brooklyn State Hospital in the New York Borough of Brooklyn and Netherne Hospital south of London—were chosen partly because their diagnostic statistics were close to the average for New York State and England and Wales respectively, and partly for practical reasons (ease of access, etc.). A series of 250 admissions was examined in each. Both first and readmissions were included but those aged under 20 or over 59 were omitted, partly to avoid the problems inherent in interviewing adolescents and the elderly, and partly to concentrate attention on the differences in the admission rates for schizophrenia and manic-depressive illness.

Every patient was examined by one of the project psychiatrists as soon as possible after admission and independently of the hospital staff. Because of the overriding need to maintain a uniform procedure on both sides of the Atlantic structured interviewing procedures were used throughout. A combination of the Present State Examination (Wing, Cooper, and Sartorius, 1972) and 200 items from the Mental Status Schedule (Spitzer, Fleiss, Burdock, and Hardesty, 1964) was used as the basic mental state interview and was followed by a semistructured history interview given both to the patient and to a relative. A 'project diagnosis' based on the nomenclature of the Eighth Edition of the *International Classification of Diseases* and the English glossary to this (General Register Office, 1968) was made on the basis of the information obtained in these interviews. The reliability of these standardized interviews was satisfactory [see CHAPTER VIII] and the American and British teams trained together and exchanged staff at intervals thereafter in order to ensure that their interviewing techniques and diagnostic criteria were the same throughout.

The 'hospital diagnoses' of these two series of patients were obtained through the normal statistical channels (the State Department of Mental Hygiene in New York and the Ministry of Health in England) and showed the familiar national differences—there were far more schizophrenics (65 per cent *v.* 34 per cent) and alcoholics (12 per cent *v.* 4 per cent) at Brooklyn and more psychotic depressives (33 per cent *v.* 7 per cent), neurotics (12 per cent *v.* 3 per cent), and personality disorders (8 per cent *v.* 1 per cent) at Netherne. The differences between the two sets of 'project diagnoses' were far smaller, however. There were still significantly more patients with affective illnesses at Netherne (47 per cent *v.* 36 per cent) and more alcoholics at Brooklyn (12 per cent *v.* 6 per cent), but the difference was reduced for every major diagnostic category and for schizophrenia it ceased to be statistically significant. A detailed comparison of the symptoms of the two series of patients [see CHAPTER XI] showed that at Brooklyn the schizophrenics tended to be more chronically ill with fewer acute symptoms but more residual defects, and at Netherne the depressives tended to be more deeply depressed and to have more typical manic-depressive symptoms, but in general the individual symptom differences merely confirmed the differences found between the two sets of project diagnoses. Partly as a result of the differences between the catchment areas of the two hospitals, and partly because of a selective loss of middle-class patients to private facilities in New York, there were prominent social and cultural differences between the two series of patients which in many ways were more impressive than the psychiatric differences. The Netherne patients formed a fairly stable and homogeneous population; they had a common ethnic and religious background and most of them were married, held steady jobs, and lived with their families. The Brooklyn patients, on the other hand, were much more diverse ethnically and culturally, and a high proportion showed evidence of social instability or failure—they were divorced or separated, unemployed, or living alone.

The consistency of the criteria on which the project diagnoses were based was tested in several ways [see CHAPTER IX], and although there were indications of minor differences between the two project teams these were trivial in comparison with the difference between the two sets of hospital diagnoses. The results of this comparison indicate, therefore, that the apparent differences in diagnosis between patients admitted to the Brooklyn State Hospital and those admitted to Netherne Hospital are largely, but not entirely, due to differences in the diagnostic criteria used by the staffs of the two hospitals.

Because of the potential importance of this finding, coupled with the difficulty of being sure that the diagnostic criteria employed by the hospital psychiatrists were representative of their colleagues elsewhere, a further comparison, described in Part 3, was carried out between samples of patients drawn from all the public mental hospitals in New York and London.

One hundred and ninety-two patients were drawn from the nine State hospitals supplying New York City and 174 from nine of the 18 area hospitals supplying Greater London. This was done by sampling methods which effectively gave all patients being admitted to public mental hospitals in the two cities an equal chance of inclusion. The same age range (20–59 years) and interviewing procedures were used as in the Brooklyn–Netherne study, except that the history interview was shortened and the interview with a relative omitted. As before, the two samples differed in a number of social characteristics which were partly a reflection of cultural differences between the two cities and partly attributable to differences in the social factors influencing hospital admission in the two. There were more immigrants in the London sample (27 per cent v. 12 per cent), but more Negroes (29 per cent v. 11 per cent), more Catholics (45 per cent v. 23 per cent), more people divorced or separated (27 per cent v. 12 per cent), and more with less than 8 years' schooling (18 per cent v. 7 per cent) in the New York sample; surprisingly, there were no social class differences between the two [see CHAPTER XIV].

The hospital diagnoses of the two series showed the same striking differences as before, with twice as many schizophrenics (62 per cent v. 34 per cent) and six times as many alcoholics (20 per cent v. 3 per cent) in the New York sample, and five times as many psychotic depressives (24 per cent v. 5 per cent) and twelve times as many manics (7 per cent v. 0·5 per cent) in the London sample. But most of these differences failed to survive the transition from hospital diagnosis to project diagnosis. Comparison of the two sets of project diagnoses indicated that there were indeed more alcoholics in the New York sample (23 per cent v. 5 per cent), and more patients with affective illnesses in the London sample (44 per cent v. 32 per cent), but for other diagnostic categories, including schizophrenia, none of the differences was significant. Indeed, if allowance was made for the larger numbers of alcoholics and drug addicts in the New York sample all differences between the two sets of project diagnoses were trivial.

As in the first study, the consistency of the diagnostic criteria of the project psychiatrists was tested, by comparing the project diagnoses with diagnoses generated by a logical decision tree analysis and by canonical variate analysis, but only minor differences were revealed [see CHAPTER XV]. The results of this second study therefore confirm those of the original single hospital comparison and indicate that, with the single exception of alcoholism, the differences between the diagnostic statistics of New York and London hospitals are largely the result of gross differences between the diagnostic criteria used by psychiatrists in the two cities. The most important of these differences is that the New York concept of schizophrenia is much broader than that used in London and embraces many patients who would be regarded by British psychiatrists as suffering from depressive illnesses, neurotic illnesses or personality disorders, and nearly all those who would be regarded as suffering from mania.

These findings are compared in CHAPTER XVIII with the results of a complementary study carried out by the project in which videotapes of diagnostic interviews with selected patients were shown to large audiences of both American and British psychiatrists. The results of the two series of studies are very similar and their implications are discussed together. Both reveal substantial differences in diagnostic usage between psychiatrists in New York and London. Because all the varieties of functional mental illness involved are defined purely in terms of their clinical features it is fruitless to attempt to decide whose diagnoses are the correct ones. It does seem, though, at least to the authors, that the diagnoses of the London psychiatrists are likely to be more useful because they are related in fairly clear and consistent ways to the patients' symptoms, whereas there is a tendency in New York for most patients, other than those with organic or addictive states, to be regarded as schizophrenics regardless of their symptoms.

The most important effect of these differences in usage is to impair communication. Diagnoses are the most vital of all our technical terms because they are the means by which we identify the subject-matter of most of our research, and if the same terms are used by different groups of psychiatrists with widely different meanings they are likely to mislead one another.

At present we do not know whether the differences revealed here between London and New York provide an accurate picture of overall Anglo-American differences. We have evidence from videotape studies that the diagnostic habits of London psychiatrists are reasonably representative of British psychiatry as a whole, but there are indications that New York psychiatrists may have a broader concept of schizophrenia than their colleagues elsewhere in the United States. If this proves to be so these studies are giving too alarming a view of the overall disparity between American and British psychiatrists. But even the available evidence makes it clear that this disparity must be substantial and, if New York does prove to be atypical of the United States as a whole, a further communication problem will be revealed between the thousands of psychiatrists in that area and their colleagues in other parts of the country.

In spite of the fact that most of the differences between American and British mental hospital admission rates have now been shown to be spurious, it is still possible that genuine differences exist in the admission rates for arteriosclerotic dementia and other disorders of old age, and still possible that community-based comparisons will reveal genuine differences in prevalence for some types of mental illness. It is our intention to explore both these possibilities in future studies.

REFERENCES

AMERICAN PSYCHIATRIC ASSOCIATION (1952) *Diagnostic and Statistical Manual of Mental Disorders* (DSM I), 1st ed., Washington, D.C.

—— (1968) *Diagnostic and Statistical Manual of Mental Disorders* (DSM II), 2nd ed., Washington, D.C.

ARNOLD, T. (1782) *Observations of the Nature, Kinds, Causes and Prevention of Insanity*, Vol. 1, Leicester.

BECK, A. T. (1962) Reliability of psychiatric diagnosis: I. A critique of systematic studies, *Amer. J. Psychiat.*, **119**, 210–16.

BRILL, H. (1966) Classification and nomenclature of psychiatric conditions, in *American Handbook of Psychiatry*, ed. Arieti, S., Vol. 3, London, pp. 3–17.

BROOKE, E. M. (1963) *A Cohort Study of Patients First Admitted to Mental Hospitals in 1954 and 1955*, Studies on Medical and Population Subjects, No. 18, London.

BROWN, G. W., BONE, M., DALISON, B., and WING, J. K. (1966) *Schizophrenia and Social Care*, London, p. 19.

BUNNEY, W. E., GOODWIN, F. K., DAVIS, J. M., and FAWCETT, J. A. (1968) A behavioural-biochemical study of lithium treatment, *Amer. J. Psychiat.*, **125**, 499–512.

BURCH, P. R. J. (1964a) Manic-depressive psychosis: some new aetiological considerations, *Brit. J. Psychiat.*, **110**, 808–18.

—— (1964b) Schizophrenia: some new aetiological considerations, *Brit. J. Psychiat.*, **110**, 818–25.

BURROWS, G. M. (1828) *Commentaries on the Causes, Form, Symptoms and Treatment of Insanity*, London.

CLARK, R. E. (1949) Psychoses, income and occupational prestige, *Amer. J. Sociol.*, **54**, 433–40.

COHEN, J. (1968) Weighted kappa: nominal scale agreement with provision for scaled disagreement or partial credit, *Psychol. Bull.*, **70**, 213–20.

COHEN, R. (1970) Objektive Klassifikationsverfahren, *Bull. schweiz. Akad. med. Wiss.*, **25**, 125–46.

COLLEY, K. M. (1960) *An Introduction to Psychoanalytic Research*, New York.

CONRAD, K. (1959) Die nosologischen Einheiten in der Psychiatrie, *Z. ges. Neurol. Psychiat.*, **150**, 8–9.

COOPER, J. E. (1967) Diagnostic change in a longitudinal study of psychiatric patients, *Brit. J. Psychiat.*, **113**, 129–42.

COPELAND, J. R. M., COOPER, J. E., KENDELL, R. E., and GOURLAY, A. J. (1971) Differences in usage of diagnostic labels amongst psychiatrists in the British Isles, *Brit. J. Psychiat.*, **118**, 629–40.

ESSEN-MÖLLER, E., and WOHLFAHRT, S. (1947) Suggestions for the amendment of the official Swedish classification of mental disorders, *Acta psychiat. scand.*, Suppl., **47**, 551–5.

ESQUIROL, E. (1838) *Des Malades Mentales*, Paris, p. 398.

EY, H. (1954) La classification des maladies mentales et le problème des psychoses aigues, *Etudes Psychiatriques*, Vol. 3, Paris, pp. 1–45.

FEINSTEIN, A. R. (1967) *Clinical Judgement*, Baltimore, Md.

FLETCHER, C. M., JONES, N. L., BURROWS, B., and NIDEN, A. H. (1964) American emphysema and British bronchitis: a standardized comparative study, *Amer. Rev. resp. Dis.*, **90**, 1–13.

FLETCHER, C. M., and OLDHAM, P. D. (1964) Diagnosis in group research, in *Medical Survey and Clinical Trials*, ed. Witts, L. J., London, pp. 23–38.

GARLAND, L. H. (1960) The problem of observer error, *Bull. N.Y. Acad. Med.*, **36**, 570–84.

GENERAL REGISTER OFFICE (1968) *A Glossary of Mental Disorders*, Studies on Medical and Population Subjects, No. 22, London.

GRIESINGER, W. (1845) *Die Pathologie und Therapie der psychischen Krankheiten*, Berlin.

GRINKER, R. R., MILLER, J., SABSHIN, M., NUNN, R., and MUNNALLY, J. C. (1961) *The Phenomena of Depressions*, New York.

GROSZ, H. J., and GROSSMAN, K. G. (1968) Clinician's response style, *J. abnorm. soc. Psychol.*, **73**, 207–14.

GURLAND, B. J., FLEISS, J. L., COOPER, J. E., KENDELL, R. E., and SIMON, R. (1969) Cross-national study of diagnosis of the mental disorders: some comparisons of diagnostic criteria from the first investigation, *Amer. J. Psychiat.*, **125** (Suppl.), 30–8.

GURLAND, B. J., FLEISS, J. L., COOPER, J. E., SHARPE, L., KENDELL, R. E., and ROBERTS, P. (1970) Cross-national study of diagnosis of the mental disorders: hospital diagnoses and hospital patients in New York and London, *Comprehens. Psychiat.*, **11**, 18–25.

HOCH, P., and POLATIN, P. (1949) Pseudoneurotic forms of schizophrenia, *Psychiat. Quart.*, **23**, 248–76.

HOCH, P., and ZUBIN, J. (1961) *Field Studies in the Mental Disorders*, New York.

HOLLAND, W. W. (1963) The reduction of observer variability in the measurement of blood pressure, in *Epidemiology: Reports on Research and Teaching*, ed. Pemberton, J., London, pp. 271–92.

HOLLINGSHEAD, A. (1965) *Two Factor Index of Social Position*, New Haven.

HORDERN, A., SANDIFER, M. G., GREEN, L. M., and TIMBURY, G. C. (1968) Psychiatric diagnosis: British and American concordance on stereotypes of mental illness, *Brit. J. Psychiat.*, **114**, 935–44.

JACO, E. G. (1960) *The Social Epidemiology of Mental Disorders*, New York.

KAGAN, A. R. (1965) Ischemic heart disease: interpretation of electrocardiograms, *Milbank mem. Fd Quart.*, **43**, 40–8.

KAHLBAUM, K. (1863) *Die Gruppierung der psychischen Krankheiten*, Danzig.

KALLMANN, F. J. (1946) A genetic theory of schizophrenia: an analysis of 691 twin index families, *Amer. J. Psychiat.*, **103**, 309–22.

KATZ, M., COLE, J. O., and LOWERY, H. A. (1969) Studies of the diagnostic process: the influence of symptom perception, past experience and ethnic background on diagnostic decisions, *Amer. J. Psychiat.*, **125**, 937–47.

KENDELL, R. E. (1968) An important source of bias affecting ratings made by psychiatrists, *J. psychiat. Res.*, **6**, 135–41.

KENDELL, R. E., EVERITT, B., COOPER, J. E., SARTORIUS, N., and DAVID, M. E. (1968) The reliability of the Present State Examination, *Soc. Psychiat.*, **3**, 123–9.

KENDELL, R. E., and GOURLAY, A. J. (1970a) The clinical distinction between psychotic and neurotic depressions, *Brit. J. Psychiat.*, **117**, 257–60.

—— (1970b) The clinical distinction between the affective psychoses and schizophrenia, *Brit. J. Psychiat.*, **117**, 261–6.

KENDELL, R. E., COOPER, J. E., GOURLAY, A. J., COPELAND, J. R. M., SHARPE, L., and GURLAND, B. J. (1971) The diagnostic criteria of American and British psychiatrists, *Arch. gen. Psychiat.*, **25**, 123–30.

KRAEPELIN, E. (1887, 1927) *Psychiatrie*, 2nd and 9th eds., Leipzig.

KRAMER, M. (1961) Some problems for international research suggested by observations on differences in first admission rates to the mental hospitals of England and Wales and of the United States, in *Proceedings of the Third World Congress of Psychiatry*, Vol. 3, Montreal, pp. 153–60.

—— (1969a) Cross-national study of diagnosis of the mental disorders: origin of the problem, *Amer. J. Psychiat.*, **125** (Suppl.), 1–11.

—— (1969b) Statistics of mental disorders in the United States: current status, some urgent needs and suggested solutions, *J. roy. statist. Soc.*, **132**, 353–407.

KRAMER, M., POLLACK, E. S., and REDICK, R. W. (1961) Studies of the incidence and prevalence of hospitalized mental disorders in the United States: current status and future goals, in *Comparative Epidemiology of the Mental Disorders*, ed. Hoch, P., and Zubin, J., New York, pp. 56–93.

KREITMAN, N. (1961) The reliability of psychiatric diagnosis, *J. ment. Sci.*, **107**, 876–87.

LEIGHTON, A. H., LAMBO, T. A., HUGHES, C. C., LEIGHTON, D. C., MURPHY, J. M., and MACKLIN, C. B. (1963) *Psychiatric Disorder among the Yoruba*, New York.

LEWIS, A. J. (1946) Ageing and senility: a major problem of psychiatry, *J. ment. Sci.*, **92**, 150–70.

LEWIS, N. D. C., and PIOTROWSKI, Z. A. (1954) Clinical diagnosis of manic-depressive psychosis, in *Depression*, ed. Hoch, P., and Zubin, J., New York, pp. 25–38.

LIDZ, T., FLECK, S., and CORNELISON, A. R. (1965) *Schizophrenia and the Family*, New York.

LLOPIS, B. (1954) La psicosis unica, *Arch. Neurobiol.*, **17**, 3–41.

LORR, M., and KLETT, C. J. (1967) *Inpatient Multidimensional Psychiatric Scale*, Palo Alto.

MAGGS, R. (1963) Treatment of manic illness with lithium carbonate, *Brit. J. Psychiat.*, **109**, 56–65.

MASSERMAN, J., and CARMICHAEL, H. T. (1938) Diagnosis and prognosis in psychiatry, *J. ment. Sci.*, **84**, 893–946.

MENNINGER, K. (1963) *The Vital Balance*, New York.

MEYER, A. (1917) The aims and meaning of psychiatric diagnosis, *Amer. J. Insan.*, **74**, 163–8.

MEYER, J. E. (1961) Diagnostische Einteilungen und Diagnosenschemata in der Psychiatrie, in *Psychiatrie der Gegenwart*, ed. Gruhle, H. W., *et al.*, Vol. 3, Berlin, pp. 130–80.

NEUMANN, H. (1883) *Leitfaden der Psychiatrie*, Breslau.

NOYES, A. P. (1953) *Modern Clinical Psychiatry*, London.

ØDEGAARD, Ø. (1945) The distribution of mental diseases in Norway, *Acta psychiat. scand.*, **20**, 247–84.

—— (1946) A statistical investigation of the incidence of mental disorder in Norway, *Psychiat. Quart.*, **20**, 381–99.

OLDHAM, P. D., PICKERING, G. W., ROBERTS, J. A. F., and SOWRY, G. S. C. (1960) The nature of essential hypertension, *Lancet*, **i**, 1085–7.

PARKES, C. M. (1963) Interhospital and intrahospital variations in the diagnosis and severity of schizophrenia, *J. prev. soc. Med.*, **17**, 85–9.

PASAMANICK, B., DINITZ, S., and LEFTON, M. (1959) Psychiatric orientation and its relation to diagnosis and treatment in a mental hospital, *Amer. J. Psychiat.*, **116**, 127–32.

POLLOCK, H. M., and MALZBERG, B. (1937) Trends in mental disease, *Ment. Hyg. (N.Y.)*, **21**, 456–65.

PRICHARD, J. C. (1835) *A Treatise on Insanity and other Disorders Affecting the Mind*, London.

RAECKE, J. (1910) *Grundriss der psychiatrischen Diagnostik*, Berlin.

RAO, C. R. (1948) The utilisation of multiple measurements in problems of biological classification, *J. roy. statist. Soc. B*, **10**, 159–93.

REDLICH, F., and FREEDMAN, D. (1966) *The Theory and Practice of Psychiatry*, New York.

RIPLEY, H. S. (1967) Psychiatric interview, in *Comprehensive Textbook of Psychiatry*, ed. Freedman, A. M., and Kaplan, H. I., Baltimore, Md., pp. 491–9.

SANDIFER, M. G., HORDERN, A., TIMBURY, G. C., and GREEN, L. M. (1968) Psychiatric diagnosis: a comparative study in North Carolina, London and Glasgow, *Brit. J. Psychiat.*, **114**, 1–9.

—— (1969) Similarities and differences in patient evaluation by U.S. and U.K. psychiatrists, *Amer. J. Psychiat.*, **126**, 206–12.

SCADDING, J. G. (1967) Diagnosis: the clinician and the computer, *Lancet*, **ii**, 877–82.

SHEPHERD, M. (1957) *A Study of the Major Psychoses in an English County*, London.

SHEPHERD, M., BROOKE, E. M., COOPER, J. E., and LIN, T. (1968) An experimental approach to psychiatric diagnosis, *Acta psychiat. scand.*, Suppl. 201.

SIMON, R. J., GURLAND, B. J., FLEISS, J. L., and SHARPE, L. (1971) The impact of a patient history interview on psychiatric diagnosis, *Arch. gen. Psychiat*, **24**, 437–40.

SLATER, E. T. O. (1935) The incidence of mental disorder, *Ann. Eugen. (Lond.)*, **6**, 172–84.

SPITZER, R. L., and ENDICOTT, J. (1968) Diagno: a computer program for psychiatric diagnosis utilising the differential diagnostic procedure, *Arch. gen. Psychiat.*, **18**, 746–56.

SPITZER, R. L., FLEISS, J. L., BURDOCK, E. I., and HARDESTY, A. S. (1964) The Mental Status Schedule: rationale, reliability and validity, *Comprehens. Psychiat.*, **5**, 384–95.

SPITZER, R. L., ENDICOTT, J., FLEISS, J. L., and COHEN, J. (1970) The Psychiatric Status Schedule: a technique for evaluating psychopathology and impairment in role functioning, *Arch. gen. Psychiat.*, **23**, 41–55.

SVENDSEN, B. B. (1952) Psychiatric morbidity among civilians in war-time, *Acta jutlandica*, **24**, Suppl. A.

THURNHAM, J. (1845) *Observations and Essays on the Statistics of Insanity*, London.

WARD, C. H., BECK, A. T., MENDELSON, M., MOCK, J. E., and ERBAUGH, J. K. (1962) The psychiatric nomenclature: reasons for diagnostic disagreement, *Arch. gen. Psychiat.*, **7**, 198–205.

WEINSTOCK, H. (1968) The role of classification in psychoanalytic practice, in *Classification in Psychiatry and Psychopathology*, ed. Katz, M., Cole, J. O., and Barton, W. E., United States Public Health Service Publication No. 1584, Washington, D.C., pp. 62–72.

WHARTON, R. N., and FIEVE, R. R. (1966) The use of lithium in the affective psychoses, *Amer. J. Psychiat.*, **123**, 706–12.

WILSON, M. S., and MEYER, E. (1962) Diagnostic consistency in a psychiatric liaison service, *Amer. J. Psychiat.*, **119**, 207–9.

WING, J. K., BIRLEY, J. L. T., COOPER, J. E., GRAHAM, P., and ISAACS, A. D. (1967) Reliability of a procedure for measuring present psychiatric state, *Brit. J. Psychiat.*, **113**, 499–515.

WING, J. K., COOPER, J. E., and SARTORIUS, N. (1972) *Instruction Manual for the Present State Examination and Catego*, London.

WINOKUR, G., CLAYTON, P. J., and REICH, T. (1969) *Manic-Depressive Illness*, St. Louis, Mo.

WORLD HEALTH ORGANIZATION (1963) Expert Committee on Health Statistics: Eighth Report, *Wld Hlth Org. techn. Rep. Ser.*, No. 261.

—— (1966) *Published National Statistics on Mental Illness in Europe*, Copenhagen.

—— (1968) Morbidity Statistics: Twelfth Report, *Wld Hlth Org. techn. Rep. Ser.*, No. 389.

ZELLER, A. (1844) Bericht über die Wirksamkeit der Heilanstalt Winnenthal, *Allg. Z. Psychiat.*, **1**, 1–79.

ZUBIN, J. (1967) Classification of the behaviour disorders, *Ann. Rev. Psychol.*, **18**, 373–401.

INDEX OF SUBJECTS

INDEX OF AUTHORS

N